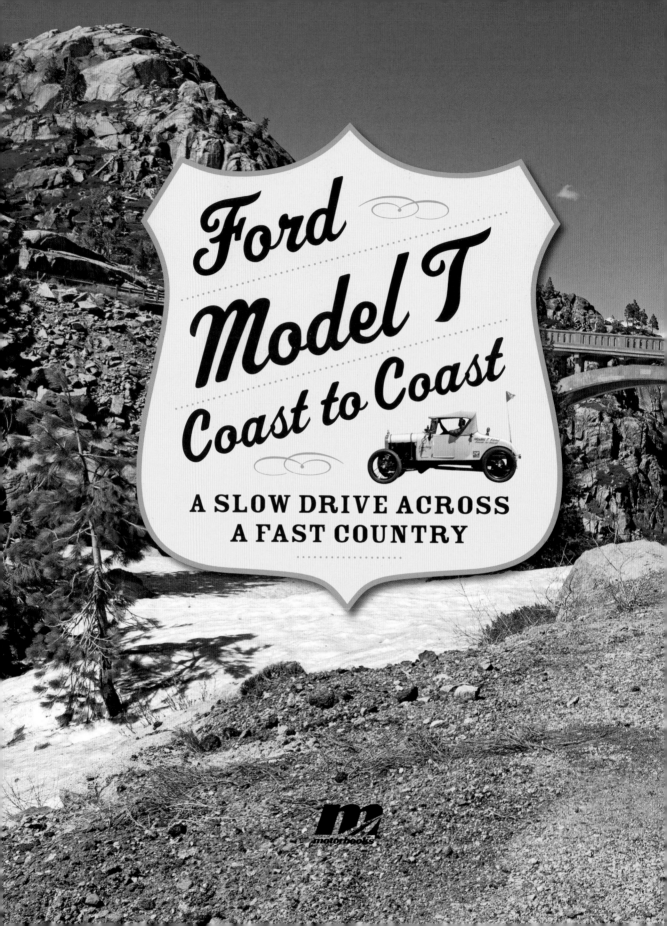

Ford Model T

Coast to Coast

A SLOW DRIVE ACROSS A FAST COUNTRY

motorbooks

TOM COTTER

PHOTOGRAPHY BY
MICHAEL ALAN ROSS

FOREWORD BY
HENRY FORD III

TO SKIP, A CAR GUY TO THE END.
YOU WOULD LOVE THIS BOOK.

Brimming with creative inspiration, how-to projects, and useful information to enrich your everyday life, Quarto Knows is a favorite destination for those pursuing their interests and passions. Visit our site and dig deeper with our books into your area of interest: Quarto Creates, Quarto Cooks, Quarto Homes, Quarto Lives, Quarto Drives, Quarto Explores, Quarto Gifts, or Quarto Kids.

First published in 2018 by Motorbooks, an imprint of The Quarto Group, 401 Second Avenue North, Suite 310, Minneapolis, MN 55401 USA. T (612) 344-8100 F (612) 344-8692 www.QuartoKnows.com

Motorbooks titles are also available at discount for retail, wholesale, promotional, and bulk purchase. For details, contact the Special Sales Manager by email at specialsales@quarto.com or by mail at The Quarto Group, Attn: Special Sales Manager, 401 Second Avenue North, Suite 310, Minneapolis, MN 55401 USA.

10 9 8 7 6 5 4 3 2 1

ISBN: 978-0-7603-5946-4

Library of Congress Cataloging-in-Publication Data

Names: Cotter, Tom, 1954- author.
Title: Ford Model T coast to coast : a slow drive across a fast country / by Tom Cotter ; photography by Michael Alan Ross ; foreword by Henry Ford III.
Description: Minneapolis, MN : Motorbooks, an imprint of The Quarto Group, 2018. | Includes bibliographical references and index
Identifiers: LCCN 2017048192 | ISBN 9780760359464 (hc)
Subjects: LCSH: Automobile travel--United States. | Ford Model T automobile. | Lincoln Highway. | United States--Description and travel.

Classification: LCC GV1024 .C67 2018 | DDC 796.70973--dc23

Acquiring Editor: Zack Miller
Project Manager: Alyssa Lochner
Art Director: Cindy Samargia Laun
Cover Design: Faceout Studio, Spencer Fuller
Interior Design and Layout: Silverglass Design

On the endpapers: Krasovski Dmitri / Shutterstock

Printed in China

Contents

· · · · · · · · · · · · · ·

Acknowledgments

. . . .

Andy Beckman, Zack Miller, Madeleine Vasaly, Nathan Edwards, Brad Phillips, Vivian Phillips, Classic Car Club Manhattan, Bob Meade, Nat Ierardi, Glenn Palmer Smith, Carl Magnusson, Pete Stout, Mike Vaughn, Rich Johnston, Diane Southall Taggart, Erin Jones, Shelly Dunno, Earl and Rainie Sonntag, Derrick Blake, Jeff Blair, Joyce Blue, Daniel Campbell, James Jaynes, Dan and Jodie Vandenheede, Christopher Woodson, Sandy Huemann-Kelly, Meredith Grossman, Cierra Steinbach, Brian Martin, Gray Irwin, Phillip Reinhardt, Austin Hiebert, Jared Thurston, Mitch Cowan, Josh Shircliff, Darrell and Rosie Crouse, Mark Anderson, Kyle Bond, Dwight Bond, Dona Smith, Riley Smith, Laura Graham, Blue Offutt, Kayla Banas, Tyler Boren, Jacob Hamblin, Noble Glines, Jordan Boren, Andy Suciu, Scott Pruett, Matt Ryan, Maya Beneli.

And of course, my wife, Pat Cotter.

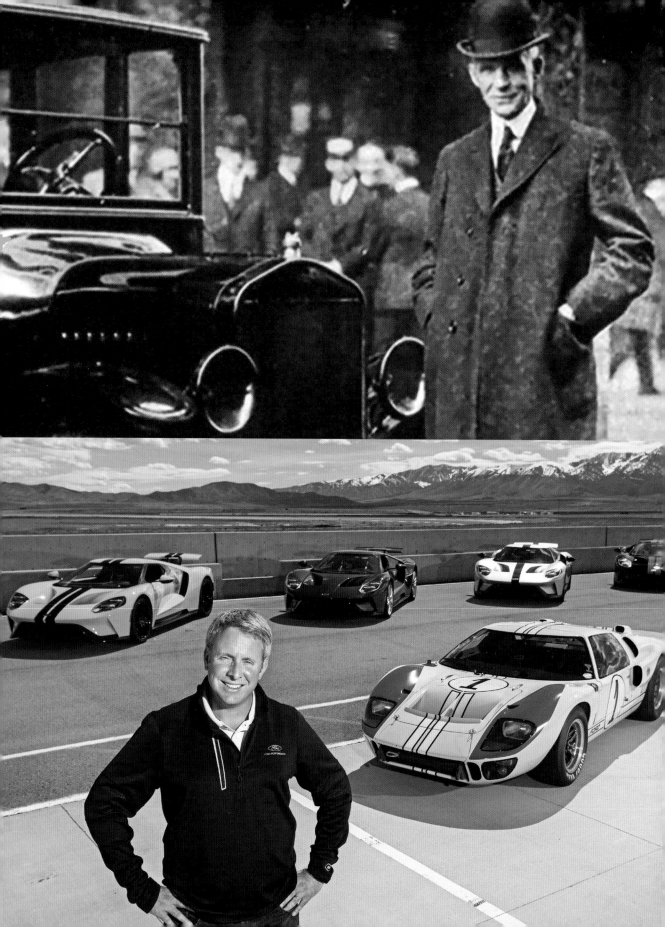

Foreword

. . . .

My great-great-grandfather Henry Ford was a man of vision and ideas. But perhaps his greatest vision was to design, engineer, and build a car that everyday Americans could afford and use. He wanted to put the world on wheels.

When he had this vision, cars were mainly for the wealthy, and people rarely traveled great distances from their homes because of a lack of affordable transportation.

The Model T changed all that.

He said, "I will build a motor car for the great multitude . . . constructed of the best materials, by the best men to be hired, after the simplest designs that modern engineering can devise . . . so low in price that no man making a good salary will be unable to own one—and enjoy with his family the blessing of hours of pleasure in God's great open spaces."

And that's exactly what he did. From 1908 to 1927, thanks to his refinement of the modern assembly line, more than 15 million Model Ts were built, changing not just the automobile industry, but literally the world itself, allowing people to go and see places they only could have dreamed of before.

It's safe to say the Model T is still one of the most iconic vehicles in our company history. And the fact that, more than one hundred years later, it's estimated that some 200,000 still exist around the world, tells you how much people still love and revere the car.

This book, the story of Tom Cotter and company's modern-day trip across America in the Model T, is just another chapter in the history of this legendary car, and I hope you will enjoy it.

HAPPY TRAVELING!

Hy Ford III

OPPOSITE TOP: Henry Ford and his Model T. *Ford Motor Company Archive*

OPPOSITE: Henry Ford III with the original GT40 (foreground) and four examples of the new Ford GT in the background. *Ford Motor Company Archive*

Introduction

. . . .

When I was young, I was only interested in speed, fast cars, and getting there quickly. The future was in my windshield, and I wanted to conquer it.

Part of my hyper vision was probably due to my Type A personality, but I wasn't alone in my affliction; it was simply part of post–World War II youth culture, my generation.

Now that youth is in my rearview mirror, I truly enjoy taking the slow road. Not that I don't still enjoy fast cars, but I've come to appreciate how things were done back in the day.

"Getting there" was important, but how we got there was equally important.

The journey became as important as the destination.

Thus, this book.

The subtitle sums it up best: *A Slow Drive across a Fast Country*. Driving a nearly hundred-year-old car across a hundred-plus-year-old road just because.

Meeting the people and seeing the sights of the thirteen "flyover" states crossed by the Lincoln Highway became a quest, and it took twelve months just to iron out the logistical details.

I promise it was worth every inch of our 3,707-mile trek.

The slow road is rapidly becoming an endangered species. In our hurried world, most folks opt for the fast, direct route rather than traveling the slow, winding roads. That's too bad, because the fast roads bypass all that is unique about America. And soon, I'm afraid, driverless cars may be making most of the routing decisions for us. Sure, the built-in GPS system will get us to our destinations efficiently, and it will reroute us around traffic congestion and accidents, but in the process it will also bypass the little treasures we can discover in out-of-the-way places.

With that loss of control, I fear we will lose some of our freedoms as well. Freedom to make our own choices—where to drive, where to lodge, where

to participate in recreational opportunities. If driverless cars make all our decisions, we have lost the freedom of choice.

This adventure, though, will allow us to visit a forgotten America—one accessed along a path plotted by human minds, not a computer. Using an atlas and a textbook, we will decide exactly where we want to travel each day, not be guided by a digital voice.

I made this journey not just for me, but for you, too. I'd be willing to bet that at least one million folks out there would have traded places with me in that tiny cockpit next to my codriver, Dave Coleman, if given the chance. If you're one of those people, this book is for you.

I hope reading about this century-old form of travel from sea to shining sea will get your gears turning toward plotting your own adventure.

And the real star of this adventure was our trusty Model T, the *Something Special*, which did not experience a mechanical breakdown even once!

Eastern 1 ▶ Standard Time

Meet our partner in this cross-country adventure, our 1926 Ford Model T speedster, nicknamed the *Something Special*. Did we bite off too much? Would *Something* be reliable enough to get us to the West Coast?

1. Thankfully, President Donald Trump did not delay the start of our trip. We had been making plans for the better part of a year, scheduling a 9:00 a.m. departure on May 7, 2017, from the intersection of Broadway and Forty-Second Street in Midtown Manhattan so we could make a quick escape from New York City. This spot, the eastern terminus of the famed Lincoln Highway, would be the launching point for our Ford Model T drive from the Atlantic to the Pacific.

Sunday mornings are special in New York. As someone who used to live there, I know it's a time to get out early and experience the city without the sidewalk crush, blaring horns, and snarled traffic. Of course, some of the Sunday-morning people haven't actually woken up early; they are wandering the streets, still partying from the night before.

So a Sunday morning was the only realistic time to consider. Driving such a primitive vehicle through Manhattan—dodging potholes, taxicabs, and commuter traffic—at any other time could have been fatal.

Our pretrip planning was going well until a couple of days before our scheduled departure date. My New York–based brother, Peter, sent me a text: "Trump is coming to town this weekend."

Rats. Wherever the president traveled on weekends (mostly to his Mar-a-Lago resort in Palm Beach), demonstrations broke out and traffic became snarled for hours. Trump Tower, on Fifth Avenue and Fifty-Second Street, was not too far from our Midtown jumping-off point. Would his presence postpone our plans?

Luckily not, as it turned out. After receiving Peter's warning, I kept a wary eye on the news and was relieved when it was announced that Trump had decided not to visit his Manhattan property that weekend after all. Instead, the president would be spending the weekend at his Bedminster, New Jersey, golf club.

One bullet dodged.

2. Four of us—photographer Michael Alan Ross; my codriver, Dave Coleman; the Model T's owner, Nathan Edwards; and I—spent our last night before the trip in Weehawken, New Jersey, at a hotel just across the Hudson River from Midtown. Michael had flown in from San Francisco, Dave and Nathan trailered the T up from West Virginia, and I'd come from Kansas. We had all been busy for the past several weeks, trying to tie up any loose ends in our personal lives before departing. We all arrived at the hotel by midnight and shared a celebratory beer before hitting the sack. We had an early wake-up call, and it was one of those nights of restless sleep, when six hours seemed more like twenty minutes.

The alarm went off at dawn. We quickly packed, went down to the parking lot, and unloaded the T from its trailer. Dave drove it through the Lincoln Tunnel and into Manhattan while I was in the passenger seat; Michael followed us in a support vehicle provided by Ford Motor Company, a 2017 Escape. Nathan rode into Manhattan in the Escape. Michael would drive the new SUV, loaded with his camera gear, our luggage, and one new Model T spare tire while I took turns piloting the T with Dave, who had actually owned it before selling it to Nathan a couple of years earlier. Nathan himself would have loved to join us if he could have taken time away from his job at an auto restoration shop. Instead, he would drive Dave's truck and trailer back to West Virginia. We promised to keep him involved in the trip as much as possible, calling him frequently and sending photos along the way.

3. Because I suspected we wouldn't be able to park on the street for more than a few minutes before being chased away by the NYPD, part of my planning was to hunt down a location where friends and family could gather before we hit the highway. I anticipated a throng of well-wishers roughly the size of the Beatles' 1965 Shea Stadium concert (estimated at 55,600) to see us off.

In the end, my friend Brad Phillips—who works with Hagerty Insurance and is probably the most "wired" person I know in the world of old cars—arranged permission for us to gather at the Manhattan facility of the Classic Car Club, located behind the Jacob Javits Center and right along the Hudson River. It was perfect: a cool automotive event space populated with both new and classic sports cars and featuring a deck overlooking the river. Our guests could begin arriving at 8:00 a.m., and we'd have plenty of room to talk about the car and our trip for an hour or so before our sendoff.

My crowd estimate was only off by 55,590.

People passing by—pedestrians, runners, cyclists, and street vendors—loved seeing our Model T, the likes of which is seldom seen in New York City (or anywhere, for that matter) these days.

In no time, it was time to hit the road.

We said our goodbyes, departed the Classic Car Club, and nervously took our vintage vehicle to the streets. It was now real. Dave would be driving the T, Michael and Nathan following in the Escape. Traffic was still manageable.

Our Official Bon Voyage Committee. Moments before we departed from Classic Car Club Manhattan, friends and relatives gathered for a photo before we drove out into New York City traffic. From left to right: Glenn Palmer Smith, Carl Magnusson, Nathan Edwards, Dave Coleman, Brad Phillips, Vivian Phillips, Tom Cotter, Nat Ierardi, Bob "Minibike" Meade. Michael Alan Ross is, as usual, taking the photo.

What looks out of place in this photo? Here we are driving from our Hudson River starting point toward the eastern terminus of the Lincoln Highway, the road that would be our home for the next few weeks.

The Model T does not have an odometer, so I'd be using the Escape's odometer to keep track of our mileage since both vehicles would be traveling together. We zeroed out the Escape's trip odometer.

Ready, set, and we're off!

Dave drove from the Classic Car Club just a few blocks to Times Square. Let the miscalculations begin. We quickly realized our plan to shoot a photo of the car in front of the Lincoln Highway sign wouldn't be possible; the intersection had been closed to vehicular traffic and transformed into a pedestrian walkway. A nice idea for walkers, but not so great for transcontinental travelers.

Time for Plan B: we double-parked our vehicles along the curb on one of the most congested roadways in the modern world while Michael and I ran to snag a photo of the sign by itself. Unfortunately, the Model T would not be in the picture, but at least there would be a photo to document the start of our pilgrimage.

We dashed back to the cars before they were towed and eased our way along the first mile of the Lincoln Highway—the entire length of the Highway in New York state.

4. Times Square was a common launch point for automotive endurance contests at the dawn of motorized transport. By the turn of the twentieth century, New York City was already the media and cultural center of the United States, so for adventurous motorists who sought the biggest publicity pop, "the City" was a natural location to wave the green flag. At the time the first cars hit American roads, however, the famous intersection was called Longacre Square; it was changed, appropriately, when the *New York Times* moved its publishing headquarters there in 1904. Thus, it became the (New York) Times Square. In 1908, six cars lined up in Times Square and began one of the most legendary auto endurance contests of all time: the New York–Paris Race, in which participants were to race across the United States, drive across the frozen Bering Strait from Alaska to Russia, then jam on to Paris. There was a snag, however: Alaska proved completely impassable, so participants loaded their cars onto ships destined for Japan. There, they began driving again, through Asia, Russia, and the rest of Eastern Europe. The winning car, a 1907 Thomas Flyer driven by George Shuster and Monty Roberts, finally took the checkered flag in Paris 169 days and 22,000 miles after leaving New York.

The race generated a huge amount of publicity about America's virtually nonexistent road system. Several years later, construction of the Lincoln Highway began—and it would have its starting point right where the New York to Paris race had begun.

Certainly our own New York departure met with much less pomp and circumstance when compared not just to that of the Paris racers but that of Emily Post, who, while on assignment for *Collier's* magazine, departed from the same location in 1915. The writer and author, famous for her etiquette advice, had been assigned to write a story about driving the Lincoln Highway coast to coast. All of her high-society friends, dressed in their Sunday finest, gathered in Times Square to wish Emily good luck while the Princess of Proper sat high up in the back seat of her car wearing a grand bonnet and holding a bouquet of violets. Her son, Ned, drove the car through Manhattan while her poor cousin, Alice, sat almost hidden from view beneath a huge pile of luggage reportedly sufficient for an around-the-world cruise. I couldn't find any evidence on the type of car the trio drove, only that it was of English origin.

While planning her trip, Post asked her travel agent about the best route to California and was promptly answered, "Union Pacific." Nonetheless, Post and her two-person crew departed from the same Broadway and Forty-Second Street intersection as we had.

She, of course, had different priorities than Dave and I. For one thing, no matter what the conditions of the roads (which were mostly dirt or mud), she required Ned to pull the car to the side each day for afternoon tea, complete with pastries. Because the Lincoln Highway was barely passable in some areas, the undercarriage of Post's car was damaged by rock outcroppings when they finally reached the western United States. And finally, in Winslow, Arizona—a good bit south of the Lincoln Highway—she told Ned she had had enough. Post loaded her car onto a train and had it shipped to California, where it was repaired as she and her party enjoyed an Arizona resort.

Post finally arrived in California, although probably not as quickly nor as cleanly as she might have imagined. We are fairly sure, though, that she never missed her afternoon tea.

In 1913, when the Lincoln Highway was newly completed, commuters traveled across the Hudson River by ferry boat from the Manhattan terminal at Forty-Second Street to the Port Imperial terminal in Weehawken, New Jersey. That ferry, a steamship, first connected New York to New Jersey in 1912, just one year

Somehow I don't think the H&M store existed at the intersection of Broadway and Forty-Second Street at Times Square when the Lincoln Highway was established in 1913. This has been the official starting location for Lincoln Highway travelers ever since.

earlier. It kept a hectic schedule, with a boat departing every five or ten minutes, depending on the time of day.

There is still a ferry from New York to Weehawken operating today, but it is now only for passengers and takes a slightly different route. Departing from New York at Thirty-Eighth Street, it crosses the river diagonally to a modern terminal on the New Jersey side almost directly across from the aircraft carrier USS *Intrepid* Sea, Air, and Space Museum.

The most direct route for vehicles exiting Manhattan for New Jersey today is to pass through either the Lincoln Tunnel or the Holland Tunnel. We decided to take the former. Of course.

A Hudson River tunnel was first conceived in 1806 by Col. John Stevens, a resident of nearby Hoboken, New Jersey, who believed a wooden tube could be installed along the river bottom. The first to be built, the Holland Tunnel, was installed in 1927 at a cost of $48 million and became the first underwater vehicle tunnel in the United States. That first year, 8.7 million vehicles commuted between New York and New Jersey for a toll fee of 50 cents. Ten years later, the Lincoln Tunnel was constructed on the approximate route of the Port Imperial Ferry, becoming the Lincoln Highway's spiritual successor, although the use of the name Lincoln is purely coincidental.

In 2017, it took us just minutes to putt-putt through the Lincoln Tunnel and enter New Jersey, our second state. Within just a few blocks, we turned onto Pershing Road, the Lincoln Highway, and were on our way. California was certainly just around the corner.

5. I had been on a crazy schedule prior to this trip, flying into Newark from Kansas, where I had been participating in the annual advisory board meeting for McPherson College, where I have been part of the school's auto restoration program since 2013.

The school offers a four-year bachelor's degree in automotive restoration that requires students take not only academic courses such as accounting and marketing, but also restoration-specific courses such as upholstery, metal fabrication, machining, and painting. It's an amazing program and will hopefully ensure that old cars will still be enjoyed and kept roadworthy long after old farts like me retire to that big junkyard in the sky.

While I was in Kansas, I spoke to a group of students about my upcoming trip. They volunteered to perform a "pit stop" on our Model T as we passed through Lincoln, Nebraska, about four hours north of the McPherson campus. I hoped we could make it happen.

After giving a presentation Saturday morning about my book *Cuba's Car Culture* with the book's coauthor, Bill Warner, I quickly shuttled to

Wichita to catch an eastbound jet in anticipation of this westbound journey. En route to Newark, I glanced out the airplane's window as we passed over states at 600 miles per hour, country that I would soon be crossing at 30 or 40 miles per hour.

Who knew what the next few weeks would bring? Not being able to predict in advance exactly how long the trip would take, given the car's low speed and potential for mechanical breakdowns, I followed the advice of others who have traveled the highway and booked my return flight for May 28—twenty-one days after our May 7 departure.

6. "Why?" was the question I heard most often when I told friends about my upcoming trip.

The easy answer was that driving a Model T across the United States has long been on my bucket list. I've been an old-car enthusiast since elementary school, and even though I've never owned a Model T Ford, the car's history, ruggedness, and simplicity have always intrigued me. I thought a coast-to-coast adventure in a century-old vehicle would be one of the milestone automotive events of my life. But, like many well-intended bucket-list entries, I had figured that it would probably never actually happen.

Then I met Dave Coleman.

Dave and I both race vintage sports cars, and we met in 2016 at Summit Point Motorsport Park in West Virginia, a nice little road course in the far eastern corner of the state. At the time, he was racing his Porsche 911 and I my 1964 Corvette. The circuit is about six hours from my home in North Carolina but only three minutes from Dave's.

I was intrigued by the cars he drove to the track and parked in the paddock. In the morning, it was a turbocharged Hudson Hornet; in the afternoon, he drove a Model T speedster.

"You've got unusual taste in cars," I told him. We introduced ourselves and quickly realized that we both shared a similar taste for eclectic vehicles.

"When you have a minute, I'll show you what I have at my house," he said. Later that day, we commuted in his Model T speedster just a mile up the road. There he showed me buildings and storage containers filled with Porsches, Ford Falcons, an MGA, at least one Studebaker, a couple of interesting fiberglass kit cars, a 1957 Corvette, a 1957 Thunderbird, and probably a dozen or more other cars that I can't remember. Standing next to Dave's Model T after touring his collection, I mentioned that it had always been a dream of mine to drive one across the United States.

"Me too," he said.

That wasn't the response I'd expected. Could I have met another wacko with the same insane desire to traverse the country at a speed roughly half as fast as cars along an Interstate highway? Amazingly, I had, and we started plotting together.

I was able to convince my publisher, Zack Miller at Motorbooks, that I believed a trip like this was worthy of a book.

"I can't believe I'm the only person who is intrigued with making a trip like this," I told him. "But most people have time constraints that I don't have. I'll be writing this book for them." He was convinced, so the true planning began.

NEW JERSEY DINERS

Pity the youth who were brought up to believe hamburgers come from McDonald's. Obviously they don't live in New Jersey.

I grew up going to the Howard Johnson's restaurant on Veterans Memorial Highway in Sayville on Long Island, where the head cook was the father of a friend of mine, Bob "Mini Bike" Meade (now my brother-in-law). It may not have been a diner by the strictest definition, but it was close. In high school, Bob and I would frequent the place once a week for the all-you-can-eat clam dinners or our other favorite, the open-face turkey sandwich with cranberry sauce, mashed potatoes, and gravy.

What is it about diners that makes them so welcoming? Perhaps it's that they offer comfort food, often twenty-four hours a day. Breakfast served around the clock? No problem. Roast beef, fried chicken, meat loaf, BLTs, vegetables, and all the fixings. Fresh pies in a dozen flavors.

Many aren't particularly clean or attractive, and both the interior and exterior design are usually outdated by at least two decades, but the dining experience is more like eating in someone's kitchen than in a restaurant. They are generally not part of a chain, instead owned and operated by a family. The food is mostly prepared on a grill, and even if "white collar" customers may eat there, it is a blue-collar dining experience.

Diners are most popular in the Northeast and Midwest, although famous diners exist in all parts of the country. Coffee is a staple, and diners are popular with truck drivers if there is sufficient parking out back. Desserts are generally a specialty, with scoops of ice cream served in little metal bowls, ice-cream sundaes, and homemade pies. Most diners still prepare hand-blended milkshakes.

Oh, and those hamburgers—they are amazing. At the best diners, the beef is thick, juicy, and usually oversized for the bun. You can order one as rare as you like. (Try that in a fast-food restaurant where the chopped meat comes in fifty shades of gray.) Lettuce and tomato are good additions, and a nicely melted slice of golden American cheese is placed squarely in the center of the patty. Ask for extra napkins right up front. And because I'm from Long Island, my burgers are garnished only with ketchup. Never mustard. Mustard is meant for hot dogs and most sausages, and it better be spicy.

What I'm saying is a New Jersey diner hamburger is a monument to American cooking. I once had a conversation with Thomas Keller, chef, restaurateur extraordinaire, and owner of both Per Se in New York and the French Laundry in Yountville, California, where people have been known to make reservations six to twelve months in advance. We were discussing fine food, exotic ingredients, and culinary presentation when he stopped and said, "Do you know what my favorite food is? A hamburger."

But there is a more complex answer to the oft-asked "Why?" that I didn't have time to relate to friends when questioned about this trip. The fact is, I consider this adventure to be the Last Road Trip. Our world is changing at an insane pace, and nowhere is that more true than in the transportation sector.

At the turn of the twentieth century, a confrontational dynamic was building between horse-and-buggy owners and the drivers of those damn horseless carriages. "They stink and they're noisy and they scare my horses," a typical farmer might say. "My hens haven't been laying eggs since my neighbor bought a Model T."

A revolution was brewing, and you can bet those loyal to genuine horsepower believed that automobiles were only a passing fad. But Henry Ford said that his original Model A, which he built in 1903, could do everything a horse and buggy could do—accommodate two people on a bench seat in the open air, have stiff springs and a short wheelbase—while producing the power of eight horses from its two-cylinder engine.

Needless to say, the horseless carriage won the battle, and for more than a century, cars have given America, and much of the world, mobility like we had never experienced before.

But we are at the cusp of another revolution, and now I'm one of numerous horseless carriage owners who are complaining. The end of the automobile era as we know it is nearly upon us, and the age of driverless cars looms on the horizon. It's too late to put the brakes on. Machines are becoming our bosses.

More and more aspects of our lives are being shaped and controlled by machines. FedEx and UPS drivers are constantly monitored for efficiency in their routes—one only need to see one of those delivery drivers sprinting in and out of their truck to know that Big Brother is watching. The brainpower behind those huge Amazon warehouses around the country is provided by machines, with humans temporarily providing the arms and legs until that function can be mechanized as well. In a TED Talk I recently heard, MIT Professor Eric Brynjolfsson noted that employees are both rewarded and reprimanded by their machine bosses in this hyperindustrial revolution, an age where the machines will win.

In the automotive world, driving functions started to be taken away from us when the automatic transmission was introduced in the 1940s, more so when they became the transmission option of choice in the 1950s. Today, automatics have all but put the standard transmission business out of business.

When I recently visited a Porsche dealership, I saw that every car on the showroom floor had an automatic gearbox. When I asked the salesman about it, he told me that less than 5 percent of Porsches sold today had

manual transmissions—this for one of the sportiest automakers on the planet. This is a travesty to me. I can't dance, but I can certainly do the next most complicated thing with my feet, which is operating a clutch. I'll be damned if I am going to give up that function. You'll have to pry that four-speed shifter out of my cold, dead hands.

The automatic windshield wiper was the second sign that driving an automobile was becoming a passive experience. When Robert Kearns applied for a patent for his invention of a wiper mechanism that would operate intermittently in misting or light rain, another manual function was taken out of the driver's hands.

Don't get me wrong; I use automatic transmissions and intermittent wipers as much as the next guy, but these developments were just the beginning of the dumbed-down driving experience we have today. Headlights go on by themselves and can switch from high beams to low beams automatically when another car approaches. Seats adjust themselves to accommodate other drivers in a household. My Ford F-150 pickup truck has a cruise-control function that clocks the pace of traffic in front of me and slows my truck down to their speed if needed. It also warns me of vehicles around my truck that might be coming too close. New Mercedes-Benz models can "self-drive"—steering and braking—for up to thirty seconds at a time. Some vehicles can back into tight parking spaces by themselves, and some trailer-towing trucks can now mysteriously back up by themselves, which I cannot begin to fathom because I've spent a lifetime becoming a competent trailer-backer-upper. This is apparently a talent that is no longer required to impress girls.

As I was preparing for my Model T trip, I heard a report on NPR that Elon Musk, founder of the Tesla brand, predicted that by year's end he'd be able to drive one of his cars from Los Angeles to New York without touching the steering wheel. Shivers ran up and down my spine. Certainly having computers that are smarter than people able to operate a motor vehicle has its good points—there will likely be fewer traffic accidents and fewer fatalities—but I'm going to go down kicking and screaming, just like the horse-and-buggy old timers did. Operating a vehicle allows me to exercise my mind and my limbs, which I enjoy. I don't mind thinking on my own, and certainly don't look forward to that function being taken away from me.

Interestingly enough, Henry Ford played a part in this machine-versus-man scenario when he sped up his famous assembly line little by little without his workers' knowledge. Those workers became the most disposable piece of the process, able to be substituted at a moment's notice. Suddenly the machines were in charge, driving the human element at an exhausting pace. Henry would likely be pleased with Musk's intentions.

So for me, this book is about much more than driving a ninety-two-year-old car across the United States. It's about an oncoming loss of freedom and the end of an era. When will man's decision making end?

Will future vacationers be able to take a cross-country family trip on secondary roads, like we are, or will the driverless car's GPS default to a more efficient route? Will the restaurants and hotels on the main streets of the small towns we pass through be forever bypassed in the near future? What experiences will future travelers be deprived of when hitting the open road?

By the time you are reading this, Musk's self-driving prediction has probably already taken place, and I have no doubt that it will be successful. My manual-gearbox, high-horsepower sports car could soon be relegated to the "lower 40," just like all those horses and buggies.

In New Jersey, we lapped our Model T around the once-proposed Formula 1 Grand Prix circuit in Weehawken. Funding for the race was never fully secured, but I felt a personal victory when we lapped the course in an open-wheeled car!

7. Arriving in New Jersey by 10:00 a.m. on the morning of our departure, we were right on schedule. We had avoided getting caught up in the New York City traffic, which would surely increase as tourists began lining up for the Sunday matinees on Broadway.

As soon as we arrived on the western shore of the Hudson River, I had a quick detour I wanted to take for totally selfish reasons: visiting the ferry terminal that bordered the New Jersey towns of Weehawken and West New York at Port Imperial. It wasn't only because this was where drivers on the original Lincoln Highway would catch the ferry to Manhattan before the Lincoln Tunnel was installed. In a past life, I was the president of the Port Imperial Racing Association (PIRA), an organization that sought to bring Formula 1 racing to a spectacular 3.5-mile road circuit along the New Jersey

NATHAN EDWARDS

What kind of person loans you his beloved car, especially for weeks at a time? Someone who is extremely kind and maybe a little out of touch with reality, that's who. In other words, Nathan Edwards, the man who made our cross-country trip possible. Though in fairness, he does have a fairly solid grip on reality.

Nathan truly does love his Model T, but then, he simply loves machinery. "I'm an enthusiast who loves the nuts and bolts and gears of machines," says the forty-three-year-old, who lives with his wife, Julie Bulger, in Winchester, Virginia. "In my job, I might be doing upholstery one day and rebuilding a transmission the next." Which is why his job as a restorer at the famed White Post Restorations is his ideal career.

Nathan has owned the yellow Model T speedster for about five years. He acquired it from my codriver, Dave. "Dave and I had just returned from a speedster festival at Speedway Motors in Lincoln, Nebraska. When we pulled into his yard, I saw this Model T sitting there, overgrown with weeds and with moss growing on it. It was a sad sight. I asked Dave, 'So, what are you going to do with that one?' Dave said, 'Oh, you can just take it.'"

With Dave's assistance, Nathan has modified the car over his five years of ownership, installing an overhead-valve conversion cylinder head, upgraded brakes, and more.

"I drive the car as much as I can, weather permitting," he says. "When I drive it to my job at White Post, customers ask me all the time, 'Is that your car? Boy, it needs a lot of work.'

"They just don't understand when I say that the car is finished."

So, now that the Model T is finished, are there any other projects on his bucket list?

"Dave has an old Jaguar 4.2-liter engine at his shop," Nathan tells me. "I think I'd like to build a period speedster powered with the Jag motor."

If he'd consider loaning us that car for our next trip, we could certainly get to the West Coast a lot faster.

shore. The ferry terminal would have been the start-finish line. For decades, groups had been proposing races through the streets of New York City, sometimes Wall Street, sometimes Central Park. But for whatever reason, those proposals never made it beyond the planning stages. This New Jersey race would have been different, though, following public roads along the Hudson River and up into the Palisades, a couple of hundred feet above the water. The venue would have been spectacular, fast and challenging, with a view of the magnificent New York skyline across the river. Unfortunately, that venture never panned out, and my career there lasted less than one year. But it was an amazing experience while it lasted.

When I accepted the position, it was in the hopes of being a part of one more significant motorsport project. I had spent about twenty-five years in the auto racing industry, promoting everything from NASCAR to drag racing, road racing, IndyCar, and even motorcycle racing. When I sold my agency, however, I sort of disappeared from the racing scene. I rationalized to my friends that my motorsport career ended with a comma, not a period—and I hoped that by bringing a major F1 race to the New York market, that would become an exclamation point! This was not to be, but I did have an amazing experience living in Manhattan, working on the sixty-fourth floor of the iconic Chrysler Building, and meeting Formula 1 stars like Sebastian Vettel and David Coulthard.

Now I was returning to my old stomping ground after five years, but with a car decidedly slower than an F1 racer. While we were at the Port Imperial site, we drove the Model T around the proposed 3.5-mile Grand Prix circuit. We stopped at the top of the course, a couple of hundred feet above the Hudson River, and I showed Dave and Michael the amazing views of the New York skyline. Too bad the race never happened, because it would have been one of the most spectacular road courses in the history of racing. At least by driving our fenderless Model T around the circuit, an open-wheel car had finally made a lap around America's Monaco. We had departed from our Weehawken hotel so early in the morning that we hadn't had time for breakfast, so we were famished. Luckily, New Jersey is famous for its classic greasy spoons, so we sought out the Coach House Diner along the Lincoln Highway in North Bergan, which has been in business since 1939. The sign out front promised "Good Food and Plenty of It!"

Even though it was still morning, I decided to indulge in a New Jersey hamburger, fries, and a Coke, though my colleagues opted for more traditional breakfasts. Our diner experience hit the spot, and I was sure we had ingested enough calories to go the distance in our Model T, which waited obediently in the parking lot.

When we walked outside, we found people gathered around the car, families with kids and cameras flashing. We allowed a couple of the youngsters to climb into the cockpit for photos. I wondered if we could expect this reception at every meal stop. When the crowd dispersed, we said goodbye to Nathan, who hopped into the Suburban and drove south so he could report back to work at the restoration shop. In his heart, he really wanted to join us. We really do owe him a huge thank-you for loaning us his car.

"We'll take care of it for you," I promised as we hit the road.

8. Before leaving the New York metro area, we wanted to participate in the age-old ritual of baptizing our tires. Early long-distance motorists performed this tradition before departing on a cross-country journey, driving their cars down a ramp or onto a beach and into the water in order to bless their tires in the Atlantic Ocean. Legend had it this would bring luck to the car and its occupants for the upcoming journey, regardless of how many times those tires may have been changed during the trip. Drivers have done rituals like this all over the country, regardless of what body of water marked the start of their journey. We needed all the good luck we could get, but finding a boat ramp in Manhattan was not going to be easy because of all the security put in place since 9/11.

While scouting the area before we set off, Michael had discovered a boat ramp near the Port Imperial ferry terminal that seemed perfect and called to tell me that he had the problem solved. Then he learned that a triathlon was planned for Sunday morning, the same day as our departure, which would likely make that location off limits.

We eventually stumbled upon a boat ramp in New Jersey's Liberty State Park, across the water from the Statue of Liberty and not far from the Lincoln Highway. Looking northeast toward Manhattan from this angle, it was hard to imagine the once-mighty Twin Towers of the World Trade Center, which stood like a fortress at the southern tip of the island until seventeen years ago.

The boat ramp was steep, so backing up after the tires got wet was a challenge for the T. Even though they were made of Kevlar, we didn't want to burn out the transmission bands, as Dave explained while he eased the car up the ramp. The three of us had a few moments on the shore to reflect on the significance of beginning our adventure before being whisked away by a friendly police officer.

We planned to repeat this baptismal process in the Pacific Ocean when we arrived triumphantly in San Francisco in a few weeks. Michael had already scoped out a location—we could only hope there wouldn't be a triathlon in the area.

. . . .

9. Our Model T began its life as a 1926 roadster, but Dave and Nathan souped it up in more recent years with period modifications and speed equipment: a Rajo overhead-valve conversion cylinder head, a Fish carburetor, headers, and Kevlar transmission bands. These upgrades were in addition to some of Dave's other magic touches, which increased the horsepower from the stock 20 to about 40. Functionally, the motor has been blueprinted, which means it has been machined and assembled to factory specifications with the utmost care.

Additionally, the brakes have been modified with Wilwood disc brakes in the front and hydraulic drum brakes in the rear. The original Model T brakes were not connected to the wheels at all—instead they slowed down a drum in the transmission, which, in turn, slowed down the rear wheels of the car. At a time when every car on the road was a Model T, this simple brake was likely sufficient; everyone slowed at the same gradual rate. But on this trip we would be sharing the road with modern cars equipped with amazingly efficient anti-lock braking systems. This one upgrade alone could be a lifesaver.

Our T has also been lowered on its suspension by about 6 inches, and the windshield and roof have been chopped another 5 inches, giving us a lower center of gravity and improved aerodynamics.

And finally, the T's front and rear fenders have both been removed, giving it a racy look. Back in the day, Model Ts modified like this were called speedsters, and many actually raced at county fairs around the country. Most were given names by their owners such as the *Fireball Special* or the *Blue Flame Special*—"Special" was almost always part of the name. So when Dave and Nathan were prepping the car for this cross-country trip, they wondered what to christen it.

They were stuck until Dave said to Nathan, "Well, it has to be the something *Special*."

"That's it!" Nathan exclaimed.

"What's it?" Dave asked.

"Let's call it the *Something Special*."

Before leaving the GP America racing circuit, we parked *Something* on the proposed upper straightaway. My driving partner, Dave Coleman (seated), and *Something*'s owner, Nathan Edwards, pose with the New York skyline in the background.

Before departing from the New York metro area, we participated in the century-old tradition of baptizing the tires of *Something* in the Hudson River at Liberty State Park, across from the lower Manhattan site where the World Trade Center's Twin Towers once stood.

10. As happy as we were to be on the road, driving *Something* through New Jersey was not an enjoyable experience, what with all the potholes, heavy Sunday-afternoon traffic, and too many mattress stores, nail salons, and "Bad Credit? No Problem!" used-car dealerships. We were truly in the land of Tony Soprano, *The Real Housewives of New Jersey*, and *Jersey Shore* (complete with Snooki and JWoww.)

If we had to drive 3,400 miles on roads like this, I would have turned around and gone back home. Get me outta here!

I just knew the roads in Iowa and Nebraska had to be better.

Frankly, following the Lincoln Highway through New Jersey would be difficult in any kind of car, but in the Model T it was a special challenge. I had printed instructions and an atlas, but occasional gusts of wind had them flying all over the cockpit. We got off the route several times—some might call it lost, though we'd disagree—but each time, we eventually found our way back onto the route.

Our route sheet read like this:

After the turn, look for a railroad drawbridge looming on the horizon. Al's Diner is on the left. Stay in second-to-right lane to avoid turning left onto Route 440; instead continue straight ahead. This route becomes Truck Route US 1-9 and is still called the Lincoln Highway in the current Rand McNally Road Atlas of the New York metropolitan area. Crossing the Meadowlands, look to the right for the Pulaski Skyway.

And that's just one part of a confusing set of instructions that continued on for twelve pages, all of which we needed just to get through one short, heavily congested, and confusing state!

Dave and I hoped that once we reached Philadelphia and began heading west, the route would be less complicated. "Take Highway 30 west for 3,000 miles, watch for the cactus, then turn left when you reach the Pacific Ocean." That sort of thing.

11. Driving a vintage car seems to bring out the best in other people. It's like walking a golden retriever or taking a cute baby on a stroller ride; everyone seems to notice and wants to take a closer look. Something made the people of New Jersey smile and respectfully survey the car from a distance. "Is it OK if I shoot a picture of it?" they'd ask.

But of course there is always that stern-eyed guy in a Kia looking straight ahead, obviously on a mission to Planet Starbucks. He is the type of guy who looked right through our car and showed absolutely no emotion.

How can this be? How can a person—especially someone who grew up during the Baby Boomer era, when the Beach Boys were singing about the Little Deuce Coupe or a 409 engine—show no emotion at all toward a yellow ninety-two-year-old car?

These are likely the same people who can enthusiastically stare at virtual reality all day long at a computer screen, but ignore "reality" when it's right in front of them.

12. I have a confession to make: I had not heard of the Lincoln Highway until I began planning for this trip. I knew I wanted to follow a significant east–west route, but I didn't want to use Route 66 because Michael and I had driven that road for a different book a couple of years earlier. In the course of investigating other historic routes, I stumbled across the name Lincoln Highway and it seemed to work well with our plans.

Now for some fun facts. Prior to the construction of the Lincoln Highway in 1913, driving across the United States was difficult bordering on impossible.

THE LINCOLN HIGHWAY ASSOCIATION

When Carl Fisher first conceived of a cross-country road, he called it the Coast-to-Coast Rock Highway. He convinced his friends to invest in his venture with the plea, "Let's build it before we're too old to enjoy it."

Fisher sought funding from automobile manufacturers and dealers, suggesting they commit 1 percent of their gross receipts for three years to support the project, but this concept was not well received. A congressman suggested to Fisher that the road might have more patriotic appeal if it had a name like Lincoln. Being an enthusiast of Abraham Lincoln, Fisher adopted the name Lincoln Highway for his project.

It was obvious Fisher could not plan and construct the road by himself, so in 1913, he organized a group of automotive enthusiasts and formed the Lincoln Highway Association, which was charged to "procure the establishment of a continuous improved highway from the Atlantic to the Pacific, open to lawful traffic of all description, without toll charges and to be of concrete wherever practical." The association was also tasked with collecting the $10 million in funding it was estimated to cost.

Boy Scouts chowing down while working along the Lincoln Highway. The Scouts were responsible for installing the concrete highway markers along the entire length, from New York to San Francisco. *Lincoln Highway Digital Image Collection, University of Michigan Library (Special Collections Library)*

Packard president Henry Joy not only contributed $150,000 to the Lincoln Highway cause but became president of the association as well. Joy saw his company's involvement as a means to promote his cars' durability and spent weeks on route-finding expeditions. President Woodrow Wilson sent in $5 and became the first member of the Association.

Although politicians and businesspeople in nearly every small town from New York to California wanted the Lincoln Highway to include their Main Street, it was Joy's mission and that of the Lincoln Highway Association board to keep the final route as direct as possible. By continuously "editing" the route, the highway was shortened from 3,388 miles in 1913 to 3,384 miles (1915), then 3,331 (1916), 3,323 (1918), 3,305 (1921), and finally 3,142 in 1924.

In 1927, the Lincoln Highway Association ceased active operations. Before disbanding, though, the members agreed to organize the installation of concrete highway markers at significant locations along the final route. In 1928, Boy Scouts from across the country planted concrete posts along the highway. The 7-foot posts were buried half underground, with 3½ feet exposed for motorists to use as guides. A total of 2,437 concrete markers were installed between Elizabeth, New Jersey, and Lincoln Park in San Francisco, California. Many of those markers still exist today, with others either being destroyed or swiped as souvenirs.

Henry Joy passed away in 1936, and the highway's founder Carl Fisher died three years later, but the highway they conceived continued to remain popular. In the 1939 film *Babes in Arms*, Mickey Rooney and Judy Garland sing the song "God's Country," from the 1937 musical *Hooray for What!*, which featured the road in its lyrics:

HI THERE, NEIGHBOR, GOIN' MY WAY
EAST OR WEST ON THE LINCOLN HIGHWAY?
HI THERE, YANKEE, GIVE OUT WITH A GREAT BIG THANK-EE,
YOU'RE IN GOD'S COUNTRY

Even though the highway continued to be referenced in books, magazines, and radio programs, its significance declined.

In 1956, the Federal Highway Act established limited-access interstate highways, complete with cloverleaf entrances and exits. And these new superhighways had numeric names. Interest in the Lincoln Highway further diminished until the driving public began an infatuation with roadside culture.

In 1988, Drake Hokanson wrote the book *Lincoln Highway: Main Street across America*, which renewed interest in the highway. Three years later, Iowa State University organized a photo exhibit and symposium to generate interest in documenting and preserving the Lincoln Highway.

In 1992, a new Lincoln Highway Association was formed with the intention of documenting and preserving the road and its history. Each state along the route has an all-volunteer group of representatives who maintain historical highway landmarks and act as ambassadors for interested tourists.

Henry Ford with his first car, his 1896 Quadricycle, and the 10 millionth Model T. To gain publicity for the car, it was driven on the Lincoln Highway from New York to San Francisco in June, 1924. *Library of Congress*

Motorists could get around their own towns without much difficulty, but commuting from one town to another was best accomplished by train rather than by automobile. Adventurous early drivers made their way from one ocean to another by connecting horse-and-buggy paths, woodland trails, and frequent jaunts across farmers' fields.

The idea of establishing one defined cross-country route was a unique one, and it was first conceived by Indiana entrepreneur Carl Fisher. Fisher, who also built the Indianapolis Motor Speedway, connected a series of existing roads in 1913 to become the first cross-country "highway." He sent scouts out to survey the best roads and connected them through signs and on maps. The Lincoln Highway was a collection of mostly east–west roads, nearly all of them dirt, which became mostly impassable mud during the rainy season. Travel was still tough, but it was a start.

As we know, the eastern terminus of the Lincoln Highway is in New York City's Times Square. After traversing a total of thirteen states, the route ends at its western terminus in Lincoln Park at the foot of the Golden Gate Bridge in San Francisco. From east to west, the highway passed through New York (approximately 1 mile), New Jersey (64), Pennsylvania (350), West Virginia (5), Ohio (239), Indiana (163), Illinois (179), Iowa (360), Nebraska (463), Wyoming (427), Utah (250), Nevada (490), and California (100).

Over the decades, the original Lincoln Highway route has been moved slightly both north and south; today it roughly parallels I-80, mostly as either Highway 30 or Highway 50. These days, its travelers have the option of substituting Wyoming for Colorado (351 miles). During planning for our trip, we had concerns about both states. In Wyoming, the Lincoln Highway and I-80 are the same road; on I-80 cars can legally travel 80 miles per hour, and as we know, motorists often travel much faster than the posted speed limit. We figured *Something* was good for 45 to 50, so having closing speeds of 30 mph or more had us concerned. On the other hand, if we chose to drive through Colorado, that would mean tackling the Rocky Mountains at their highest elevations. Crossing the Rockies in Wyoming would be much easier.

We still hadn't come to a decision by the time we set off. Thankfully, we had a couple of weeks before we absolutely had to choose.

I suppose the Lincoln Highway is less well known than Route 66 is because there was no popular TV show or hit song with the same name. In other words, the Lincoln Highway did not have the same good PR as Route 66.

CARL FISHER

There were many people involved in creating the Lincoln Highway, but there was only one father, Carl Fisher.

Fisher was born in Greensburg, Indiana, in 1874. He stood out from his contemporaries as being particularly innovative, energetic, and competitive, whether it was on ice skates, canoeing, or his first love, bicycling.

As a teenager he saved $600—which in 1891 was the equivalent of an average year's salary—by selling books, magazines, and newspapers to railroad commuters. He invested the money in a bicycle shop, which soon became a distributor of leading manufacturers' products. But when the automobile became popular, Fisher became a racing enthusiast, driving race cars throughout the Midwest. Despite having bad eyesight, he became a champion, and in 1904 he held the record for courses over 2 miles.

In his thirties and now wearing glasses, the man known as "Crazy Carl" retired from auto racing and became an Indianapolis car dealer. And he invested in a new product: Prest-O-Lite, a powerful, carbide-gas-powered automotive headlight that allowed for safer nighttime driving. This investment made Fisher rich.

Soon he and some friends built a little auto-racing course that you may have heard of, the Indianapolis Motor Speedway.

In 1913, the gregarious Fisher conceived the Lincoln Highway, a road that would stretch from New York to San Francisco. Frustrated, however, with the delays in funding and building the road, he voiced his complaints to the head of Packard Motor Company, Henry Joy. "Joy, the way things are going in this country, we will get the American highway system about the year 2000," he is reported to have said. At the time, the notion of a cross-country road was so bold that few thought the project could actually be built. Yet, in a couple of years, it would become the most famous road in the world.

The entrepreneur's entrepreneur, Carl Fisher. Developer of the Lincoln Highway and Indianapolis Motor Speedway, and of Miami Beach and Montauk Point. *Lincoln Highway Digital Image Collection, University of Michigan Library (Special Collections Library)*

Fisher followed up the Lincoln Highway with the Dixie Highway, which gave motorists a more direct route from Michigan to Miami. As a natural extension, he became the original developer of Miami Beach.

Fisher then set his sights on developing what he envisioned as the Miami of the North—Montauk Point on Long Island's east end. The stock market crash of 1929, though, put an end to his big dreams and developments. It seems a shame that a man with such huge ideas ended up living in a small cottage in Miami, doing work for friends.

Having lost his substantial fortune, he viewed himself as a failure toward the end of his life. He died in 1939.

Fisher was inducted into the Automotive Hall of Fame in 1971 and has been named one of the most influential people in Florida, once referred to as Mr. Miami, by the *Ledger* newspaper. Through his vision, Fisher developed South Miami, which has gone on to become one of the wealthiest and most exclusive residential areas in the United States.

With luck, this book, along with the good work of the Lincoln Highway Association, will bring additional attention to this historic route.

13. It was chillier in the afternoon than when we'd started early on Sunday morning, and Dave and I put on our jackets. And hats. And gloves. Michael, in the Escape, probably turned on his heated seats.

The sky was cloud covered, and there was a brisk breeze blowing. I hoped that as we traveled further south and west, the sun would come back out and the temperature would rise. Instead, however, rain started to fall, not enough to install the side curtains—the canvas-and-vinyl windows that Model Ts used instead of roll-up windows—but just enough to make the car's occupants feel a little yucky. Unlike in a modern car, whose windows can close at the touch of a button, putting up the side curtains requires parking the *Special*, opening the trunk, removing and assembling the steel frames and the cloth pieces, and installing the units. No doubt we'd get soaked during that long ritual, and it was just too much trouble for some minor precipitation.

Also, having no side windows made communicating with other motorists much easier. At traffic lights, many motorists gave us a thumbs-up. Some rolled their own windows down.

"What year is it?"

"1926."

"Where are you heading?"

"California."

"California? Right now? Really? Can I come?"

Despite the damp and chill, we were living the dream.

14. *Something* (remember, that's our car's name) cruised happily along with traffic once we made it onto US 1 south of Trenton. We were finally past the crowded, Walmart-infested heart of New Jersey—here the road was smooth and wide, though still fairly crowded with Toyota Camrys, Ford Fusions, and Subaru Foresters.

Just as we were getting into the rhythm of New Jersey traffic, however, *Something* sputtered and stalled.

"Out of gas," Dave said knowingly. Model Ts don't have fuel gauges, so we'd had no advance warning.

Happily, dipping our wheels into the Atlantic Ocean a couple of hours earlier apparently had given us good luck after all: we were right in front of a Shell station! I hopped out of the passenger seat, Michael parked the Escape, and a couple of kind motorists jumped out of their own cars to help push *Something* off the road and up to the gas pump.

We'd only driven 85 miles since leaving New York and had gone through a whole tank of fuel—much lower fuel efficiency than we had anticipated. We'd need to be more diligent about checking our fuel level for the rest of the trip. Without a fuel gauge, we'd use a plastic dipstick that Dave had stowed in the trunk. If we ran out of fuel in the Nevada desert, I doubt we'd be as lucky as we'd been today.

"You drove that all the way from Virginia?" a man hollered from his minivan at a traffic light, noticing our license plate. We were just about to enter Philadelphia.

"Actually, we're driving it all the way to California," Dave said.

The minivan-driving man was impressed.

15. We decided to make our first day a long driving day. We'd put a lot of miles under our belts already in order to get the heck out of Dodge (so to speak). And most of the day we drove on roads congested with families going to soccer games and shopping trips.

I prayed that the Lincoln Highway had more to offer as we headed west than what we'd experienced during these first few hours.

I had explored the historic hotel options along the highway in the days leading up to our departure, and I had my sights set on a classic little motor lodge: the Lincoln Motor Court in a town called Manns Choice, Pennsylvania. According to the books I had read, it was an authentic Lincoln Highway landmark featuring sleeping cabins built around 1939. It would be quite a slog—at least a 300-mile driving day to reach Manns Choice by dusk—and we got a little bit off track as we passed through Conshohocken, Pennsylvania. That name rang a bell. Then it came to me; old-time sports-car enthusiasts might remember this was the home of the Judson Supercharger. This bolt-on speed accessory was popular in the 1950s and 1960s and increased the horsepower of small cars such as VWs, MGs, and Triumphs. I own an old VW convertible with a Judson Supercharger mounted on the original 36-horsepower engine and can verify that the power increase it real. The label attached to the top of the turbo proudly states that it was made in Conshohocken.

But soon we were back on the Lincoln Highway and heading west.

Fuel:
11.13 GALLONS
Distance:
85 MILES

At each fuel stop, we kept track of how many miles we had driven since our last fill-up, and how many gallons of gas we purchased.

16. It was getting colder as we drove toward Manns Choice, and we hadn't seen the sun since we'd left Manhattan. With a breeze blowing and a light rain falling, the 50-degree air temperature actually felt much colder. The mist blowing through the cockpit felt like one of those misting machines that cool the crowds waiting in long lines at Disney World. Nice on a hot July day, but on this semifrigid May afternoon, not so good.

17. After four hours of driving, with just about 100 miles under our belts, we finally reached Highway 30. We would remain on this route until we reached Cheyanne, Wyoming, probably two weeks from now.

Driving toward Lancaster, Pennsylvania, passing through places with names like Kinzers and Paradise, the landscape began to look like the America I had hoped to see. We passed through quaint little burgs with authentic, healthy main streets lined in historic stone buildings and houses.

We began to see signs warning us to be aware of horses and buggies that might be sharing the road with us—we were driving through Amish country. When we stopped for gas again, it was so odd to see an Amish buggy parked at the station next to pickup trucks as the very well-dressed men and women were inside the market buying milk and bread. Even odder was the contrast of seeing a young Amish man, probably eighteen years old and dressed in his Sunday best, his buggy parked out front, buy a pack of cigarettes from a young, blue-haired clerk with a lip ring, nose ring, and tongue piercings. I wondered what was going through each of their minds as the transaction was taking place. Talk about a clash of cultures.

Soon we were driving through Gettysburg, Pennsylvania, and I felt a pang in my stomach. Here was a town with a beautiful square and coffee shops and little cafés, tidy sidewalks, and pretty homes—all of which belie its history as the site of one of the bloodiest battles of the Civil War.

When Emily Post drove on the Lincoln Highway in 1915, she decided to go north of New York City because she'd been advised that crossing the high altitudes of the Allegany Mountains might be treacherous. After driving

Fuel:
15.63 GALLONS
Distance:
158 MILES

Once we cleared the New York congestion and got into rural Pennsylvania, we occasionally came across vehicles that were even slower than ours!

Something up what locals call the "folds," a series of tall peaks and low valleys, I now know what she was afraid of.

On one elevation called Tuscarora Mountain near McConnellsburg, Pennsylvania, the Lincoln Highway rises to 2,123 feet above sea level. Now that's not tall when compared to some of the summits in the Rockies, but it is tall for the East Coast. As the road went up a steep grade, *Something* did her best imitation of the Little Engine that Could: I think I can, I think I can, I think I can. Dave kept the car in high gear, and even though we could only achieve a speed of 32 miles per hour, *Something* never sputtered or coughed.

She was proving to be quite an impressive little machine.

18. After more than twelve hours on the road, we finally arrived at the Lincoln Motor Court at 9:00 p.m. The air temperature had dropped to 36 degrees, so my first question to proprietor Debbie Altizer was whether the cabins had heat.

She assured me they did. Michael and I shared a double cabin, and Dave had a single to himself.

It had been an exhausting yet amazing first day. We had driven 324 miles, roughly 10 percent of the length of the Lincoln Highway, since leaving Times Square.

And even though the heater in the cabin worked great, I think I shivered all night. I was cold down into my bones and extremely tired. I needed sleep, and I'm sure my traveling colleagues needed the same.

Good night.

We arrived in Gettysburg, Pennsylvania, at dusk. It was hard to conceive this was the site where more Americans killed Americans than in any other battle in the Civil War.

Fuel:
21.23 GALLONS
Distance:
251 MILES

19. Checking into the Lincoln Motor Court is like checking back in time. Nine housekeeping cabins assembled in a horseshoe shape offer Lincoln Highway tourists an authentic peek into the past. The motel was built in the early 1940s and has been owned by the current proprietors, Bob and Debbie Altizer, for more than three decades. They have done an amazing job of maintaining and refurbishing one of the last cabin lodging establishments along the Highway.

"We signed the mortgage on my birthday, July 27, 1983," Debbie told us. "The place had been closed for about five years, but we heard it had been a brothel for a while before that."

I asked her what led the couple, who would have been very young at the time, to pick up their roots and move to the country to run a motor lodge.

"We lived in Alexandria, Virginia, near Washington, D.C.," she said. "Life was becoming a rat race. It was the early 1980s, and things were happening around us that we didn't like, so we wanted to escape.

"We drew a circle on a map with towns two hours from Alexandria. We looked at campgrounds and general stores, businesses we could run. We fell in love with this place and have been here ever since."

Bob and Debbie had to invest a lot of sweat equity, because even though the cabins were structurally in good condition, the carpeting, windows, and shades all needed replacement. Each cabin is decorated with period accessories, such as lamps, dressers, and chairs, with magazines from the 1950s arrayed on the nightstands. There are some modern conveniences, such as microwave ovens, refrigerators, and coffee makers, but no phones, air conditioning, or hair dryers. Until recently, there were no color TVs.

The interior walls are finished in appropriately vintage knotty-pine boards, and even though the bathrooms are very small, they get the job done. I don't think I've seen light-blue bathroom fixtures since I was in second grade, but they looked just right in this setting. Nightly rates are reasonable, with a double cabin (two people) available for $75 to $80 per night.

The Lincoln Motor Court is listed in the National Register of Historic Places and has been featured on a PBS special about the Lincoln Highway.

"We raised two daughters here," Debbie said. "One became a school teacher and the other a banker. This place has provided us with a grand life!"

We could not have chosen more appropriate accommodations for our first night on the road, and hoped that we could find more lodging of this caliber during our trip.

OPPOSITE TOP: This photo of an old Ford in front of a cabin at the Lincoln Motor Court could have been taken seventy-five years ago. It was an appropriate location to end the first day of our cross-country drive.

OPPOSITE LEFT: Proprietors Debbie (pictured) and Bob Altizer bought the Lincoln Motor Court thirty-five years ago, and have worked hard to preserve and maintain the character of their historic lodging establishment. The cabins look as though they are out of a 1940 issue of *National Geographic* magazine.

OPPOSITE RIGHT: Each room features knotty pine paneling, vintage bathroom appliances, and even vintage copies of magazines. It felt as though we were allowed to sleep in a museum for a night.

Jack Dunkle (left) and Dave give *Something*'s engine a once-over. Jack is a hot rodder, and was fascinated with the modifications Dave has performed on the Model T engine.

20.

On the morning of our second day, it was a brisk 33 degrees in Manns Choice. Yikes!

We hadn't planned for temperatures this low, and our packed clothes showed it. I didn't want to get out of bed. I was not yet ready to crawl out into the cold early dawn and climb into an unheated, drafty car at near-freezing temperatures.

But I did.

I turned on the shower and waited for it to warm up, but it never happened, so this would be a no-shower Monday. I later found out that Debbie had forgotten to turn on the hot-water heater that morning—all the hot water at the motel comes from a water heater inside her and Bob's house, and pipes channel the hot water underground from one cabin to the next. Our cabin was the fifth or sixth in line to receive hot water if it had been turned on several hours earlier.

Debbie apologized profusely, but it was really no big deal. We'd just make sure tonight's lodging had hot water before we checked in.

Because the Escape had heat, we all piled in to drive a few miles east to the town of Bedford for breakfast. Bedford, which sits in the center between Philadelphia and Pittsburgh and today is the county seat for Bedford County, was established around a trading post and settled in 1715. In 1794, Gen. George Washington marched his army through Bedford in order to put down a rebellion when a special tax was put on whiskey.

Bedford is also home of medicinal springs of mineral, sulphur, limestone, and chalybeate as well as two sweet springs. Legend

Fuel:
25.53 GALLONS
Distance:
337 MILES

has it that one mechanic in the area, who was plagued with a variety of ailments including rheumatic pains and ulcers, drank and soaked in spring water and within a few weeks was totally cured. The springs' healing ability had people flocking to the town hoping to find a cure for their illnesses. Several resorts opened to capitalize on the healing springs, but not much has happened there in the past few decades with the exception of Lincoln Highway tourism, most notably Dunkle's Gulf station and the World's Largest Coffee Pot.

Speaking of coffee, we ingested a wonderful breakfast at the Landmark Restaurant, where we were told all the locals eat. Our server and some of the diners at the counter gave us suggestions on other local sites we needed to see before moving on, specifically, you guessed it, Dunkle's Gulf and the World's Largest Coffee Pot. We obliged, hoping that the sun would warm the earth enough over the next hour or so to allow us to comfortably climb into our drafty car and continue our trek west.

While we were talking with station owner Jack Dunkle, a man who was driving by noticed *Something* and came over to give it a closer look. He said he had been an architect in Detroit earlier in his life and once had owned Henry Ford's rolltop desk. "I used it for a while, but unfortunately I gave it away. Wish I had it back again."

Before we left Dunkle's, we decided it would be appropriate to top off *Something*'s gas tank at this landmark station.

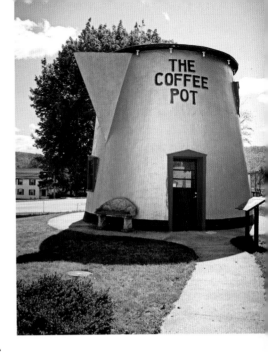

Just up the street from Dunkle's is the World's Largest Coffee Pot, another Lincoln Highway landmark. Built in 1937 as a café, it had fallen into disrepair until a restoration effort had it moved and refurbished into a tourist site.

DUNKLE'S GULF

Dunkle's Gulf service station is an amazing piece of historical automotive treasure. The art deco building was opened in 1933 by Dick Dunkle as a full-service station offering both fuel and repairs. Dick's son, Jack, still runs the family business today, pumping gas and repairing cars in the garage along with his wife, Susan. Jack told us that except for a couple of years when he was in the military, he has worked at the station his entire life.

Jack enjoyed inspecting *Something*'s engine as Dave pointed out some of the mechanical upgrades he and Nathan had made to the car. Jack told us he had a couple of old Fords as well, a Model A and a 1932 Ford, both hot rods.

Perhaps the most amazing throwback to days gone by at Dunkle's is that customers don't need to pump their own gas; an attendant does that for you! And they wash the windshield of every car.

"We still pump gas, we still repair cars, and we still lose money," Jack told us as we were leaving.

A wonderful reminder of just how good the good old days were.

FLIGHT 93 MEMORIAL

September 11, 2001, is a date that Americans of a certain generation will remember forever. Four jetliners were hijacked by al-Qaeda terrorists and used as missiles to attack American landmarks. Three of those jets hit their intended targets: two flew into the World Trade Center's Twin Towers as much of the country watched their television sets in horror, and a third jet crashed into the Pentagon in Washington, D.C.

The fourth jet, United Airlines Flight 93, never reached its target, which most likely was the United States Capitol Building. Instead, it crashed into a field near Shanksville, along the Lincoln Highway, in Somerset County, Pennsylvania. Perhaps because the plane veered off course and never hit its intended target, it received less news coverage than the other three flights. But the fact that the forty crew members and passengers on board became citizen soldiers, fighting hand to hand with the four enemy hijackers, may make it even more newsworthy.

The scheduled departure time for Flight 93 from New Jersey's Newark Airport was 8:00 a.m., but it was delayed because of heavy air traffic in the New York metropolitan area. Its intended destination was San Francisco. The flight lifted off at 8:42, just four minutes before Flight 11 crashed into the first of the Twin Towers just across the Hudson River in Manhattan. Flight 93 climbed to its cruising altitude of 35,000 feet within just a few minutes.

Routine radio communications between air-traffic control and Flight 93 ceased at 9:27 a.m., and the hijacking began just one minute later. That was when First Officer LeRoy Homer called to air traffic control, "Mayday, mayday."

By this time the other three flights had hit their intended targets, so all commercial aircraft around the country were put on high alert.

First Officer Homer and Capt. Jason Dahl fought back valiantly, but they were overpowered as hijackers took control of the aircraft's cockpit. Voice recordings reveal that by 9:31 a.m., the hijackers had taken control of the jet.

By now it was apparent to passengers and crew what was happening. Hijackers announced over the intercom that there was a bomb on board and that they were returning to the airport. Passengers and crew frantically attempted to make phone calls to family members.

One passenger, Tom Burnett, was able to communicate with his wife, who told him about the jet collisions at the World Trade Center. Until this point, passengers on board hadn't heard. He ended his call, telling his wife, "We're going to do something."

According to cell phone records, passenger Todd Beamer's wife heard him reciting the Lord's Prayer with fellow passengers, then said, "Are you ready? Okay, let's roll." Flight recorders heard screams and scuffling as a group of passengers rushed toward first class to overtake the hijackers.

At 9:59 a.m., the hijackers, aware of the passenger revolt, flew the plane erratically, banking

OPPOSITE: The breathtaking Flight 93 Memorial charts the flight path of the United Airlines jet (before it crashed into the field just beyond the walls in the distance) with these dark gray paving stones.

ABOVE: Besides Gettysburg, the most sobering site we encountered on our trip was the Flight 93 Memorial in Shanksville, Pennsylvania. Out the window to the right is where Flight 93 crashed on the morning of September 11, 2001, when passengers wrestled the controls from terrorists to prevent the plane from crashing into another building, probably in Washington, D.C.

rapidly from side to side in an attempt to keep them from entering the cockpit. Passengers and hijackers were heard fighting in the cockpit to gain control of the steering yoke. The plane plummeted into a nosedive and crashed into an empty field at about 10:03 a.m.

It is estimated that Flight 93 hit the ground at 563 miles per hour at a 40-degree angle. The impact left a crater 8 to 10 feet deep and 30 to 50 feet wide. All forty-four people on board, forty passengers and crew and four hijackers, died. Investigators found small debris, paper, and nylon as far as 8 miles from the point of impact. The voice recorder was found underground, 25 feet below the impact crater.

Years after the crash, Flight 93's intended target is still being speculated. The Capitol Building or the White House were likely targets, but Camp David is also a possibility.

People began leaving memorials near the crash site almost immediately, and several foundations were established to fund a more permanent tribute. In 2003, the federal government announced its intention to establish a permanent memorial, and a design competition was initiated.

On September 7, 2005, the commission was awarded to *Crescent of Embrace* by Paul and Milena Murdoch, one of 1,011 submissions. The National Parks Commission purchased the land from property owners for $9.5 million, and the Wall of Names opened on September 10, 2011. The visitor center opened on September 10, 2015. Both are aligned with Flight 93's flight path.

The section of the Lincoln Highway that passes near the Flight 93 crash site has been renamed Flight 93 Memorial Highway.

21. I'm a runner, so I notice hills that most people don't tend to while driving their cars. *Something* notices hills as well.

Like a runner, the Model T will be cruising along at a nice clip on a flat road, then start going slower and slower as the elevation increases. Our cruising speed so far on this trip had been 45 to 50 miles per hour, but on these inclines, *Something* will slow down to 40, then 35, then 30. The little engine's torque, though, is amazing, and never once have we had to downshift into low gear.

22. Just a few miles west of the Lincoln Motor Court, we came upon a sobering landmark: the Flight 93 Memorial.

We paused to recall that horrific day, September 11, 2001, when two commercial airliners flew into the World Trade Center and one flew into the Pentagon. One more jet got less attention because, instead of a high-profile site, it crashed into a farm field in Shanksville, Pennsylvania, right along the Lincoln Highway. This memorial was created to preserve the memory of that flight, its crew, and its passengers. A sign reads, "A common field one day, a field of honor the next."

Visiting this memorial gave me the same emotional chill as I got from the Vietnam War Memorial in Washington, D.C. I don't personally know anyone who died in Vietnam, nor do I know anyone who died on Flight 93, but visiting both these sites left me feeling like I knew all of them.

It was a beautiful day, with blue skies and the slightest of breezes, probably much like the day the crew and passengers fought with terrorists and purposely crashed into this field in order to save more lives. The jet crashed at 10:03 a.m. on September 11, the 155-foot-long jetliner reduced to scattered fragments across 40 acres.

Inside the pavilion were photos of happy faces alongside the names and biographies of the forty passengers and crew who perished that day. There were television news broadcasts on large screens that brought that whole distant morning back into focus. The building was crowded with people, but no one was talking. Everyone was silently reliving the events that had unfolded seventeen years earlier and learning about the heroes who didn't make it home that night.

I'm sure I was not the only visitor who cried at the memorial that day.

By the time we left the memorial and were back on the road, the temperature had warmed up to a balmy 40 degrees. At least we wouldn't be breaking a sweat.

23. The sign said "Walat's Famous Ham Sandwiches," which got our attention. I'd never heard of these supposedly famous ham sandwiches before, but apparently someone had, because, well, they're famous.

So we pulled into the parking lot and prepared ourselves for a sandwich that surely couldn't be beat.

Walat's, in Boswell, Pennsylvania, is a bar in probably a sixty- or seventy-year-old building that, at least at the time of our visit, still allowed patrons to smoke inside. That was an instant turn-off for me, because over the past twenty years or so, I've gotten used to eating my meals without smelling tobacco. But I needed to try one of those sandwiches, so I rationalized that it would just be like eating smoked ham.

As we waited for our food, we watched the television over the bar, which was playing reruns of *Match Game*. *Match Game*, for Pete's sake! It was 12:00 noon, and people were drinking beer and eating sandwiches and enjoying a television show that has been off the air for fifty years.

When the sandwiches were delivered, I couldn't believe my eyes. They were obscenely huge—the three of us could easily have shared one. These things were probably 4 inches tall, piled high with thick, hand-cut slices of ham. Not only could we not finish the sandwiches, we couldn't even get our mouths around them. Even Dave, who had wisely chosen a smaller version instead of the regular size that Michael and I had ordered, couldn't clear his plate.

Later, I looked up Walat's on TripAdvisor. I thought one of the reviews summed up our feelings pretty well: "What a messy, dirty bar. The huge ham sandwich was very good, but the hamburger was dry. Very reasonable prices, cold beer. Friendly bartender. Horrible rest rooms, sticky tables and torn barstools. Don't understand the popularity."

There was enough meat in that sandwich to feed a small nation! Literally pounds of thick-sliced ham was wedged into that roll. I made my best attempt to eat it, but I could only consume about half.

24. After a day and a half on the road, it was time for me to climb behind the wheel of *Something*. It would be a first for me: despite being an old-car guy my whole life, I had never driven a Model T Ford. Up to that point on the trip, I had been a passenger in our speedster, but had not yet driven it.

I had always been attracted to later V-8-powered Fords, those of the 1930s and 1940s. They were the cars I admired as a kid on the pages of *Rod & Custom* and *Hot Rod* magazines.

As my love for old cars grew, I pulled my father into the hobby too. He had no real interests besides playing his flute in front of the radio to Arthur Fiedler and the Boston Pops

Orchestra on Saturday evenings, so I started dragging him (he drove) to Early Ford V-8 Club of America meets and the annual Hershey Antique Automobile Club of America (AACA) swap meet while I was still a kid.

I suppose my father was typical of Depression dads: so totally tuned to providing the bare essentials for his family that there was never enough time or money for hobbies. No golf, no fishing, nothing. Sad.

I bought a 1939 Ford woody wagon when I was fifteen (a car I still own today), and together he and I took it apart and refinished the wood. But we didn't have the garage, money, or tools to complete the project—and as a teenager, as much as I loved my vintage wheels, I was more interested in girls, cars that ran, and going to the beach than sanding wood.

So driving old cars was not on my agenda when I was a teen. They always required too much work to make them roadworthy. I tried to make up for that when I drove the same woody across the United States with my own son, Brian, thirty years later.

But Model Ts just never hit my hot button. I suppose it was because I watched *Leave It to Beaver*, in which Lumpy Rutherford drove a 1940 Ford convertible, and it made me attracted to later cars.

So today was my chance. Dave said he could teach me *Something*'s unique method of operation. For me to have driven this car in New York or busy New Jersey traffic would have been foolish. But we were now in the country, and I had been observing Dave's pedal operation for the past 400 miles, so I was now eager to give it a try!

When I talk to young people about learning to drive manual transmissions, I try to convince them that it's like learning a new language—that these days, not too many people know how to do it. Now it was my turn to learn a new language.

Standard Model T Fords have three pedals. Nothing unusual there. Except these three pedals don't work like the three pedals on any other car. Let's start on the left: the pedal furthest to the left is not the clutch pedal but the shifter. Push that pedal all the way down and the car is in forward low gear; bring it halfway up and the transmission is in neutral. Bring it all the way to the top and the transmission is in forward high gear. This pedal takes the most time to become comfortable with and takes the place of a shift lever.

The middle pedal is for reverse. That's simple.

The pedal on the right is the brake pedal. Not that it does much, though; the brake pedal on a standard Model T doesn't engage brakes at the four wheels but instead slows down a drum in what is called a planetary transmission, which, in turn, slows down the rear wheels. I wouldn't want to trust my life on that weak system. Thankfully, Dave and Nathan felt the same way, which is why they'd installed the Wilwood disc brakes in the front and a set of homemade hydraulic brakes in the rear. And it worked pretty darn well.

Fuel:
30.73 GALLONS
Distance:
426 MILES

So that's the standard setup—only *Something* has an extra fourth pedal. All original Model Ts have the accelerator on the right side of the steering column, opposite where a blinker lever would be on a typical car. But on ours, it has been replaced by a floor pedal on the extreme right. So, effectively, this is the only pedal on *Something* that would be the same as a modern car.

There was one more "control" required to operate this car correctly: a lever on the left side of the steering column that could be confused with a blinker stalk. This controls ignition timing. Push the lever up and the ignition advances, making it easier to start. Bring the lever down just a little bit—about half an inch—and you retard the ignition, making engine run faster and smoother.

There you have it. Model T Operations 101.

I drove *Something* westbound on a rural section of the Lincoln Highway for 20 or 30 miles, then turned the controls back over to Dave. There would be lots more opportunities for me to drive this car over the next few weeks. At sixty-four years old, I don't learn new things very often these days, but I must admit that I really enjoyed learning to drive this car.

"You did excellent for your first lesson," Dave said. I took it as a compliment from an old pro like him. My hope was that by the time we arrived in California, I'd be totally fluent in this new language.

THOSE DARN CARS

The newfangled horseless carriage didn't have it easy in its earliest days. Country people, mostly farmers, were vehemently opposed to the noisy, smoky contraptions, which they criticized as being toys for the rich that scared their horses. Farmers all over America often booby-trapped routes that were frequented by cars by spreading shards of broken glass along the roadway in an attempt to blow out the fragile tires. They also half-buried rakes with the tines pointing up.

In Pennsylvania, the Farmers Anti-Automobile Association went so far as to draw up rules for automobiles to follow when traveling through rural regions:

1. Automobiles traveling on country roads at night must send up a rocket every mile, then wait ten minutes for the road to clear. The driver may then proceed with caution, blowing his horn and shooting off Roman candles, as before.
2. If the driver of an automobile sees a team of horses approaching he is to stop, pulling over to one side of the road, and cover his machine with a blanket or dust cover which is painted or colored to blend into the scenery, and thus render the machine less noticeable.
3. In case a horse is unwilling to pass an automobile on the road, the driver of the car must take the machine apart as rapidly as possible, and conceal the parts in the bushes.

Pretty severe indeed, but it illustrates just how far folks were willing to go to legislate automobiles into being functionally useless.

Folks in Pennsylvania who abhorred the automobile's arrival also took a stand against using public tax dollars to improve road surfaces. But as the price of cars started to come down—specifically the Model T, which by 1927 could be purchased for less than $300—farmers started to see the value in gas-powered cars, trucks, and tractors. In 1918, only four of sixty-six Pennsylvania counties voted against a highway bond issue, designating a staggering $50 million to build and improve state roads.

25. As far as cities are concerned, Pittsburgh isn't a bad one to bypass. The Lincoln Highway, Highway 30 in this area, becomes I-376 as it passes through the center of Pittsburgh. Despite some early rush-hour, stop-and-go traffic that afternoon, we averaged 20 to 25 miles per hour through town, and once we were on the west side of the city, we were roaring again at 53 miles per hour. Yee-haw!

Within thirty minutes, we were crossing the Pennsylvania state line into West Virginia. After New York's single mile, West Virginia has the second-fewest Lincoln Highway miles at just 5. We'd be in and out in just a few minutes, passing through the very northern corner of the state.

26. West Virginia is the latest state to be added to the Lincoln Highway system, though that was ninety years ago now. When the original route was moved slightly southwest of Pittsburgh, it came to pass through the town of Chester, and West Virginia became the route's thirteenth state.

The land where Chester now sits was owned by members of the Okehocking tribe until 1702, when William Penn had the Native Americans forcibly moved to other land in the county. The first European settlers in Chester were from Sweden, and initially named the town Finlandia. Because of its location on the Ohio River, it became a shipbuilding center during the Civil War. Interestingly, the shipyard was later repurposed as a Ford Motor Company assembly plant, which remained in operation until 1961.

The town claims that the hoagie sandwich was invented there. As a person who devours Jersey Mike's sub sandwiches, I bow down to the person or people who invented this type of cuisine, but I could find no evidence to back up Chester's claim.

Highway 30 skirts past the town center, but we decided to exit onto the traditional Lincoln Highway and take a drive through town. Most of the historic landmarks in town have disappeared, but one unique attraction remains: the World's Largest Teapot, the perfect complement to the coffee pot we'd visited the day before in Bedford, Pennsylvania.

The 14-foot-tall structure was originally constructed in Oakdale, Pennsylvania, in 1938 as a root-beer barrel. It was later moved to Chester and converted to a teapot to highlight the area's major industry, ceramics, becoming a souvenir stand that sold pottery, ice cream, and refreshments on a major intersection along the Lincoln Highway. The teapot was sold in 1947 and fell into disrepair; when the land under it was sold to a public utility in 1984, the teapot sat abandoned. In 1990, the structure was restored by local historians and moved to a site down the street from where it had sat for decades. A fence was installed around the attraction to prevent vandalism.

Nearby, where the Lincoln Highway crosses the Ohio River (again) into Ohio, was once the site of Rock Springs Park, an amusement park that opened in 1897 (on land where George Washington once camped in 1770) and closed in 1970. The park included a roller coaster, swimming pool, bowling alleys, shooting gallery, baseball diamond, scenic railway, and other assorted rides and attractions. Its original owner sold it just three years after it opened to Charles Smith, a local businessman who owned many other businesses in the Chester area and was seemingly an interesting character. Smith is said to have owned the first automobile in the town, a Stanley Steamer, and once drove it across the Ohio River itself when the water was low. He is also listed in *Ripley's Believe It or Not!* for having the East Liverpool–Chester

Gas Gauge

Model Ts have no odometer or fuel gauge, so Dave devised a dipstick out of a piece of PVC pipe that could be inserted in the fuel tank to check our fuel level. Great idea— we just weren't very disciplined in using it . . .

bridge, which he owned, rebuilt without stopping traffic. Smith took in $360,000 in toll receipts—some $6 million in today's dollars—during his last year of bridge ownership, 1938, after which he sold it to the state of Ohio. That bridge no longer exists, but the fact remains that Charles Smith must have been one heck of an entrepreneur in the little town of Chester, Pennsylvania.

27. It's amazing how much you can see, appreciate, and learn about an area by driving at a low speed. Because we were slower than most other traffic on the road, we enjoyed the sights, sounds, and smells on our drive that most of the motorists passing us in their airtight cubicles were denied. We passed people walking on sidewalks in small towns, commuting to work or perhaps to a coffee shop, some of whom yelled compliments to us about our car. And because spring was in full bloom, we could smell the freshly mowed, bright-green lawns that are typical of healthy grass that has been revived after a long winter dormancy.

Of course, driving through rural areas, we also encountered other smells. The first time it happened, I looked suspiciously over at Dave, and he looked suspiciously over at me. I wondered to myself if those World Famous Ham Sandwiches were doing a number on our stomachs.

I think we were both relieved when we passed a large cattle farm half a mile up the road.

28. This is a public service announcement: the paragraphs that follow are for gearheads only. If you are not so afflicted, please skip to the next section. Thank you.

It might surprise you to hear that driving *Something* reminded me more of driving a 1950s sports car than a nearly hundred-year-old Ford. That's because Dave, who is a Porsche racing engineer and driver, had engineered it to perfection. In other words, *Something* is not your average Model T speedster. To start, the engine has been blueprinted to race-car tolerances, cylinder-head ports matched and connecting rods balanced. Interestingly, the connecting rod and main bearings still retain the original Babbitt poured metal that was installed by Ford Motor Company in 1926.

"All the critical engine and suspension parts are fabricated from vanadium steel," Dave told me. "Those pieces were stronger than standard steel pieces, so they could be made smaller and, therefore, lighter."

Substituting the standard L-type cylinder head, a Rajo Model C overhead valve conversion has been installed on the Model T block. The name Rajo is a combination of the first two letters of the Wisconsin town where the heads were made (Racine) and the first letters of the man who designed and manufactured the heads (Joe Jagersberger). The Rajo head doubles the standard Model T horsepower from 20 to 40.

The standard cast-iron pistons in the engine have been swapped for high-compression aluminum units, increasing the compression ratio from about 3.6:1 to 5.1:1 and reducing the engine's internal reciprocating weight.

Something's camshaft retains the stock lift and duration but has been advanced 7 degrees from stock. The distributor has been converted to an electronic ignition, and the car has a modern alternator.

These modifications allowed us to cruise comfortably at 53 to 55 miles per hour, at least 10 to 15 miles per hour faster than a stock Model T. But they aren't the only changes Dave and Nathan have made over the years.

They continued their modifications in the suspension by lowering the center of gravity by 6 inches from stock. This was achieved in the front by installing a 3-inch dropped front axle and rearching the leaf spring and in the rear by moving the rear axle over the rear spring, giving it an underslung profile. The steering has received a deadlink. Tube shocks have been installed in the front and Armstrong lever shocks from an MGA have been installed in the rear.

To install the front disc brakes we have already discussed, Dave fabricated caliper brackets and machined the front hubs to accept disc rotors. He also machined his own hydraulic rear brake cylinders out of round billet aluminum stock. *Something* is probably one of just a few Ford stock Model Ts with four-wheel brakes.

To aid in aerodynamics, owner Nathan chopped the windshield, and thus the convertible top, by 4 inches, which means Dave and I weren't able to wear top hats, but could scoot down the road a lot quicker.

Besides, we'd left our top hats at home.

BELOW: The key to *Something*'s horsepower is this Rajo overhead-valve conversion, which functionally doubles the engine's horsepower from 20 to 40.

BOTTOM: You're not likely to see too many Model T Fords with disc brakes! In an effort to make this car as safe in modern traffic as possible, Dave and Nathan installed disc brakes in front and hydraulic drum brakes in the rear.

29.

It was 6:30 p.m. on Monday when we passed into our fifth state, Ohio. Not that we were trying to break any speed records, but the car was running so well that it was easy to put miles under our belts. *Something* had not sputtered once.

We were hoping to find another historic hotel to spend the night—we'd been recommended a couple of historic lodges that we were keeping in mind, but it would all depend on timing. No matter how perfect the hotel, if we passed it at 10:00 in the morning, we weren't going to stay there.

30.

I remember exactly the first time I entered Ohio. It was in the summer of 1978, and my wife, Pat, and I were driving our rebuilt 1971 Datsun 240Z on our first cross-country tour. We were young, married less than two years, and I was between jobs. Pat was an elementary-school teacher, so she had the summer off.

Neither of us had ever been out of the Northeast, so we were excited about seeing new parts of the country. The furthest west I had ventured prior to this trip was Hershey, Pennsylvania, and I couldn't quite smell the Pacific Ocean from there. We wanted to get as far as possible from Long Island, where we had both been born and raised, and the New York metropolitan area, and we wanted to do it as quickly as possible. So we got up very early on a July day and left at about 4:00 a.m.

That first day, we drove long and hard. I vividly remember reaching the Ohio state line on I-80, where the sign read, "Welcome to Ohio, Gateway to

Earl Sonntag collects 1955, '56, and '57 Chevys, and proudly showed us this original-paint, three-tone 1955 four-door with only 21,000 miles on the odometer.

the Midwest." I got chills—we'd made it. Soon we'd be at the Pacific Ocean drinking Coors beer (which at the time was only available west of the Rockies).

I was in for a rude awakening when I found out we still had more than 2,000 miles to go. The impatience of youth.

And boy was I disappointed when I finally drank that first Coors beer.

. . . .

31. All of us slept like we were dead on Monday night—I don't think I moved at all once I was under the covers. We woke to a magnificent sunny and cool morning, 37 degrees, and I could tell it was going to be a beauty.

Rainie (pictured) and her husband, Earl Sonntag, operate Palmantier's Motel in Minerva, Ohio. The restored establishment started out as the Palmantier Tourist Home in 1875.

We had overnighted at Palmantier's Motel in Minerva, Ohio, a town with humble beginnings. It all began in 1818 when a surveyor, John Whitaker, purchased 123 acres to construct a log mill. The mill became a town, and in 1833 he named it after his niece Minerva Ann Taylor.

Local legend has it that the French held nearby Fort Duquesne in the 1760s. George Washington led two thousand British troops to take it over, but the local Native Americans warned the French, who abandoned their compound. They took with them 1 ton of gold, which was to be used for the French soldiers' payroll, carried by ten pack horses. Washington led his forces to a successful overtaking of the fort, but not the gold. The general and his British troops continued to chase the French, who, in anticipation of being captured, buried their treasure "at the fork of three springs." One mile west of the supposed location, a rock was placed in the fork of a tree. Over the years, many have attempted to locate the treasure, but to this day nothing has ever been discovered.

When we rolled into Minerva Monday evening, we discovered a treasure all its own in the form of Palmantier's. It was late, so we didn't take much time to appreciate our lodging before hitting the hay, but it was clean as a whistle and decorated nicely in a car-and-motorcycle motif.

One thing we did notice was that each room had its own garage— *Something* was going to be spoiled tonight.

Palmantier's Motel is run by Rainie and Earl Sonntag, proud innkeepers who enjoyed telling us about their business. This was definitely not a chain hotel. The beds and pillows were so comfortable, I could have stayed in bed all day, but I rustled myself out and made my way to the office to talk with Rainie. She told me that her last name, Sonntag, means Sunday in German. Earl had been a plumber and Rainie worked in the local school district before they bought the hotel for $100,000.

Erin Jones serves up meals at the Country Café in East Canton. We had a great time meeting locals and telling them about our Model T adventure, and were surprised and delighted when one of them paid for our breakfast.

"It was originally built in 1875 as the Palmantier Tourist Home," Rainie told me. "It started as a boarding house. Then the hotel was built in 1940. This place was in horrible condition when we bought it; it had been neglected and closed for years."

The couple quit their day jobs, rolled up their sleeves, and started cleaning, painting, and repairing. They were lucky; within their first year in business, the gas and oil business in their area exploded (so to speak), and workers started to take up residence at the motel on a long-term basis.

It took the couple three years to get the property back in shape. "But we'll never be finished," Rainie said. "Earl put in a new toilet just last week."

"We have a lot of old-car groups that come through when they travel the Lincoln Highway," Earl told us. Earl himself collects '55, '56, and '57 Chevys. He has six, including a 1955 three-tone, four-door sedan with just 21,000 miles on the odometer.

"It was purchased new at the local Chevy dealer here in town, and it really never left," he said.

32. After leaving Palmantier's, we drove into the nearby town of East Canton for breakfast. As Michael and Dave walked into the Country Café, I headed through the parking lot and toward a police officer who was sitting in his squad car with a radar gun in his hand. I just wanted to see how his morning was going and take the opportunity to learn more about how his radar equipment worked.

I introduced myself to Chief Derrick Blake, a twenty-year veteran in the Village of East Canton. Chief Blake said he had admired *Something* as we pulled into the parking lot.

"I don't think you need to worry about us speeding through town in that car," I told him.

The speed limit on the road he was patrolling was 35 miles per hour. I asked him how much leeway he usually gives motorists.

"I won't let my guys ticket anyone driving slower than 50 miles per hour," he said. "It's been my standard since I joined the force."

The chief's soft spot for speeders probably comes from the fact that he is a lifelong drag racer.

"I race a 1974 Vega with a 406-cubic-inch small-block that turns 10.75 in the quarter mile," he told me. "But I usually run at the local one-eighth-mile strip, where it turns 6.75. I race every Sunday from spring until October.

"I can't paint cars, but I built everything else on the Vega myself. I'm just a poor guy with a welder."

I had a great time talking with Chief Blake, but I was getting hungry. Not surprisingly, however, by the time I met up with Dave and Michael in the restaurant, those two scoundrels had already eaten and were chatting up Erin Jones, the pretty lady who worked the counter.

The Country Café seemed to be the favorite breakfast spot for area residents; just about every seat was occupied when I walked in.

"Is that your old car out there?" someone asked. So we told the morning diners about our New York–to–California adventure. Several diners who were particularly enthused walked into the parking lot for a closer look at *Something*.

When we finished eating breakfast and attempted to pay, we were told that one of the other diners had already picked up our check. Nice people, these East Canton folks.

Chief Blake was still in the parking lot when we headed outside. I introduced Dave and Michael, and the Chief agreed to help us with some funny photography.

Before we left, I asked Chief Blake whether there were any speed traps between East Canton and Indiana we should be aware of.

"None that I know of," he said. "Most people think this is a speed-trap town."

I, for one, know that's not true.

As we got ready to continue on our westward journey, Chief Blake told us to drive carefully.

"Thanks for stopping by," he said. "You guys made my day."

You made ours too, Chief. Thanks.

East Canton Police Chief Derrick Blake posed for a prank photo, pretending to give Dave a speeding ticket. Somehow, I don't think Dave would be smiling had this been a genuine citation. Behind is Chief Blake's police cruiser with lights flashing.

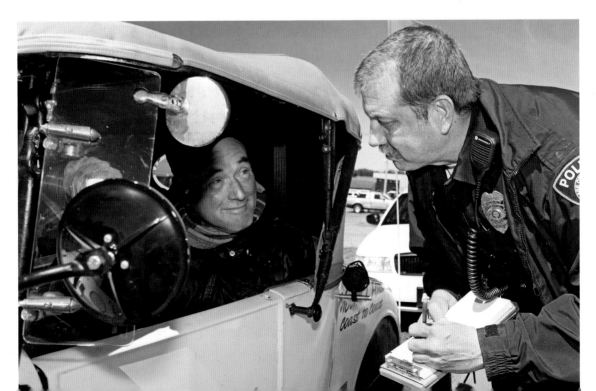

Workmen building a bridge on the Lincoln Highway between Bucyrus and Upper Sandusky, Ohio. *Lincoln Highway Digital Image Collection, University of Michigan Library (Special Collections Library)*

33. When I visit the Midwest, I feel like I'm coming home again. Mind you, I have never lived in the Midwest, but there is something so wholesome about Midwesterners. The people are friendly, the towns are authentic, and the food is good. The air is clean, and you can drink the water right out of the tap.

I was first exposed to the Midwestern way of life while I was working with NASCAR teams. The agency I founded, Cotter Group, was lucky enough to secure John Deere as a sponsor for the Busch Grand National car driven by Chad Little. The marketing executives at Deere hoped the sponsorship would increase sales of their tractors and industrial equipment to commercial customers.

During that period, I attended meetings at the company's corporate headquarters in Moline, Illinois, and at satellite facilities throughout the region such as Horicon, Wisconsin. I'd come home from these trips and tell Pat that I had met the nicest people who were so satisfied and humble. It was a far cry from the hustle and bustle New York environment in which we had both grown up.

34. We made a point of getting off the "big" Highway 30 and onto the many Lincoln Highway spurs as often as possible. The smaller routes added a bit of time to our drive, but they fulfilled our desire to take the slower roads. The newer, straighter, faster routes cut through the clutter and allow eighteen-wheelers to get to their destinations more efficiently, but the clutter for me is the best part. Low-speed travel is what it's all about.

We joked that these original Lincoln Highway routes could certainly have been the inspiration for poet Robert Frost's "The Road Not Taken," which was written three years after the Lincoln Highway was developed.

Since the high-speed bypasses have been installed, folks who live along the Lincoln Highway are probably thankful to see less traffic in front of their homes. But the poor businesses have been hurt immensely. No longer do commuters frequent the local cafés, hotels, and other businesses that were established decades earlier. These days, visitors go to the more convenient Starbucks for their coffee and Hampton Inn for their overnight stays.

The Lincoln Highway spurs are the gems of the open road, exposing travelers like us to these small businesses that are so often overlooked by interstate drivers. At the Country Café, we saw freshly baked pies under glass covers. They served real eggs, not the generic powdered egg mix stored under warming lamps like some fast-food establishments. Similarly, Palmantier's Motel, run by Rainie and Earl, had been a terrific lodging experience. And the proud innkeepers enjoyed spending time with us and telling of their business. Try that in a chain hotel.

35. Just west of Wooster, Ohio, along a section of Highway 30, *Something* gave a big cough, sputtered, and died.

"Hmmm," Dave said. "Out of gas again."

Luckily we were still coasting and only a mile from an exit. Dave let it roll in neutral for a while, then popped it into high gear. The engine sputtered back to life for a few moments, giving us just enough momentum to coast through the exit, across the bridge, and into a gas station on the eastbound side.

The 10-gallon tank took 10.5 gallons at the pump. Empty indeed. But it showed that we could achieve 19 miles per gallon, which was pretty good. This was the second time we had run dry on fuel, and the second time we had lucked out by making it into a gas station.

Without a fuel gauge or an odometer in the Model T, we had to either stop every now and then to check the fuel level with the Dave's homemade PVC-plastic dipstick or forget about it until it started to cough. The latter was not the best idea.

The only gauges on *Something*'s dash are an ampere meter and an accessory ambient-temperature thermometer. Henry Ford probably felt more information might confuse his consumers.

The generation of cars after the Model T provided drivers with just-the-facts-ma'am data: fuel, amps, oil pressure, water temperature, and speed, all displayed on easy-to-read analog gauges. Then, in the 1960s, motorists were further coddled by the invention of the appropriately named idiot light. These little devices notified drivers with a warning light when it was too late—when their engines were already out of oil or water, or the generator had stopped producing voltage, or they were overheating.

Fuel:
41.23 GALLONS
Distance:
624 MILES

Driving with such limited gauges made me realize just how spoiled we've become with all the information telegraphed to us through the slick digital dashboards of today's cars. Fuel system data tells us how many gallons remain and how many miles we can expect from that remaining fuel. GPS devices tell us where to go, cell-phone voice commands allow hands-free calling, and satellite radio brings us entertainment programming from outer space. The modern dashboard has gone from being a device meant to give us basic analog information to one that resembles the control panel of Star Trek's USS Enterprise. But then again, I'm an analog kind of guy; just give me the facts, ma'am.

Still, we needed a more concrete plan to deal with fuel before traversing through states like Wyoming, Utah, or Nevada, any of which could potentially leave us stranded with a long walk to find a gas station. Dave came up with a solution: stop for fuel every three hours.

Seemed like a good idea to me.

36. There is something so authentic and wonderful about a paper map. On a road trip, there is nothing I enjoy more than charting on an old-fashioned atlas where I am, where I am going, and where I've been.

Many folks don't have much use for paper maps anymore, preferring to use the GPS function on their cell phones. The problem I have with those devices is that they simply guide you to a destination without allowing you to understand how you got there. "Go 36.2 miles, then turn left." You get the idea.

Our plan was for me and Dave to become totally unplugged on this trip—we'd leave our cell phones and GPS units at home and travel like motorists did one hundred years ago. Though we ultimately cheated and brought some electronic devices as backup, we still tried to dial back technology as much as possible, attempting to replicate as much of the simplicity of early motorists as we could.

I'm generally a tactile kind of guy who enjoys sitting down with a book, newspaper, magazine, or an atlas rather than using the digital equivalent. When I taught public relations at Belmont Abbey College, I'd regularly bring newspapers into the classroom to show students examples of effective story placement. One day a student asked, "Where do you even buy those? I think my dad used to read them." I felt like such a dinosaur.

Perhaps the day is approaching when we won't be able to purchase a newspaper or magazine. Or an atlas.

Then again, apparently a lot of the younger generation are rediscovering and enjoying a back-to-basics movement. Witness the resurgence of vinyl records, craft-brewed beer, and homegrown home-renovation projects, all experiencing increased popularity with people my son's age.

OPPOSITE: One of the hazards of operating a Model T without an electric starter motor was having the engine crank "kickback," which sometimes broke the operator's hand, wrist, or arm. This motorist's right wrist is about to be tended to by a medic. *Library of Congress*

Driving a basic car fits right into this mindset. My son, Brian, enjoys nothing more than driving his twin-turbo, third-generation Mazda RX-7. I equate back-to-basics driving—driving by the seat of my pants—to flying without instruments or radio, instead navigating strictly with charts.

I'm reminded of a terrific book, *Flight of Passage* by Rinker Buck. It's a true story about two teenagers, the author and his older brother, Kern, who restored an old Piper Cub in the family barn over the winter of 1966. The following summer, they flew it from New Jersey to Los Angeles and back. The Buck brothers had no instruments or radio, using charts, highways, geography, and their own intuition to navigate their way to the West Coast.

Fuel:
45.89 GALLONS
Distance:
721 MILES

Compared to the Buck brothers' primitive journey of fifty years ago, we were thoroughly modern. Even though we used an atlas and Brian Butko's brilliant book *Greetings from Lincoln Highway: America's First Coast-to-Coast Road* to chart our course, we had a cell phone and a GPS just in case we got into trouble.

The atlas we used on the trip was the same one I'd used on all the road trips I've taken since 2008, when I purchased it at a truck stop: the Roadmaster Deluxe United States, Canada, and Mexico road atlas. What sold me on it were the large-format state maps and the tough plastic front and back covers, which would prevent it from falling apart prematurely like so many other atlases I've owned in the past. A decade later, here I was still using it, though by now

it was looking pretty tattered. Some of the pages were detaching from the binding, and half the state of Virginia had totally fallen out. My old atlas may not look very tidy these days, but it still gets the job done, thank you.

37. We decided to stay in Ohio one more night before crossing into Indiana, and Van Wert seemed like a nice little burg. Dave, Michael, and I checked into the Holiday Inn Express at dinnertime and ventured downtown for nourishment.

There we met Shelly Dunno, who has lived in Van Wert her whole life. These days she bartends at the Black Angus restaurant on Main Street, a road also known as the Lincoln Highway.

"We used to have the largest county fair around, but not anymore," lamented Shelly. "And we had the largest peony flower farms in the country— we even had a peony parade and a peony queen—but no more."

Van Wert is also the site of the first county library in the United States, but Shelly didn't mention that. In addition, it was home to the only factory in the world that made Liederkranz cheese, a particularly pungent strain that used to be produced there by Borden.

"People around here just don't do anything on Friday nights anymore. It's just a dead, dying town."

But while we were sitting at the bar, we also struck up a conversation with Chuck Steele, a retired Van Wert County judge, whose outlook was considerably more optimistic.

ANY COLOR YOU WANT . . .

For a hundred years, the rumor was that Model T Fords could be purchased in any color, as long as it was black. That was not the entire truth, though; of the more than 15 million Model Ts built during the car's nineteen-year lifespan, only 11.5 million were finished in black.

In early 1909, Model Ts were painted red, gray, or dark green. From mid-1909 to early 1911, they were either dark blue or dark green, colors that, because they were extremely dark, sometimes appeared to be black. From late 1914 through August 1925, all Model Ts sold were black. Beginning in late 1925, with Model T sales plummeting, Ford began offering the car in a variety of colors again.

The rumor was that the black finish—which was actually varnish, not paint—dried faster than other colors, allowing the cars to be completed faster. Studies show, however, that they all dried in about the same time.

Historians believe that black was used more often because it is durable and less expensive than the alternatives. Also, areas of the car that received the most abuse (the fenders and the running boards, for instance) continued to be finished in black even after the main bodies were painted in colors again.

"We raised ten million dollars' worth of private funding for a new performing arts center that we gave to the high school," he said. "The Boston Pops, Bernadette Peters, and REO Speedwagon will be performing there this season."

That's as well-rounded a lineup as I've ever heard.

"We also restored the domed ceiling in the old 1876 courthouse that had been hidden for years beneath a false ceiling. "Ours is a nice little family town. I think we have about fifteen thousand people in the county."

Once Steele left for home, we continued our conversation with Shelly. She's the mother of two sons, a fourteen-year-old and a seventeen-year-old; the elder is enrolled at the University of Akron and hopes to become a quantum physicist. I was impressed and also somewhat intimidated, not knowing what quantum physicists do.

We devoured some of that terrific steak that only seems to be available close to the source in the Midwest. Unfortunately, Liederkranz cheese was not offered as a garnish.

Soon, Shelly's husband Shawn showed up and Shelly introduced us. Like his wife, Shawn is a Van Wert native. He owns a local machine shop and is the founder of an air ambulance and transport service based in Greenville, Tennessee. One of the other Black Angus diners heard us talking with Shawn about old cars and decided to join the conversation.

"Is that your Model T parked out there at the curb?" he asked.

"Yeah, we're driving it across the United States from New York to San Francisco on the Lincoln Highway," I told him.

"You know, in the next town, Ohio City, is the site of the first automobile accident in the United States in 1891," he said. "You guys should go over there and check it out. Also, out on Highway 24, the gangster John Dillinger apparently was once involved in a gunfight."

The sun was rapidly setting, so even though I knew Dillinger, like me, was a diehard Ford enthusiast, we only had time to visit one landmark before calling it a day, and we decided on the accident site.

I guess Ohio City should be a destination among car people, but I must admit that I'd never heard of the place before. When the city was founded in 1876, it was called Van Wert Junction. Six years later the name was changed to Enterprise, Ohio, but that caused confusion because there was already a town in Ohio called Enterprise. In 1890, fourteen years after it was founded, the town council met and voted to change the town's name for the third time to Ohio City. That one seemed to stick, because it has remained the same for more than a century.

Our bartender at the Black Angus restaurant was Shelly Dunno, who has lived in Van Wert, Ohio, her entire life, and has seen the town shrink as industries have pulled out over the years. Others we met, though, said the town is rebounding.

Upon further research, Ohio City claims to be the site not only of the first car accident, but also of the first successful automobile manufacturing plant.

And one man, John William Lambert, was responsible for both. Lambert is credited with producing the first gasoline-powered automobile in the United States. He must have been a busy guy in 1891, because he was building cars and crashing them at the same time! This first accident occurred at the intersection of South Liberty and West Carmean Streets. Legend has it that Lambert and passenger James Swoveland were driving in one of his vehicles when they hit a tree root, which caused the car to careen out of control and smash into a hitching post.

I wonder how insurance companies would accept an excuse like that today.

Injuries were minor, according to the Ohio History Connection, the state's historical society. Lambert, unfazed, went on to patent more than six hundred inventions, mostly affiliated with the foundling auto industry.

If only I could have interviewed Lambert in order to get his side of the story. Sadly he has been dead since 1952.

In honor of Lambert and his place in automotive history, Ohio City hosts the annual Lambert Days on the third full weekend in July. The festival includes a whiffle-ball tournament, softball game, parade, Texas hold'em tournament, and car show. Although it would be appropriate, there is no word about an annual demolition derby also being held in Lambert's honor during the festivities.

Before departing Van Wert, we stopped by a large mural painted on one of the older buildings along Main Street. While we staged a photo with *Something* in front of the mural, a woman employed by the Van Wert Area Chamber of Commerce came over to talk. She told us about some new projects and partnerships that were taking place across the city.

"New industries are moving into town," she said. "The future could not be brighter." Just some more of that Midwest optimism.

38. Before we checked out of the Holiday Inn Express in Van Wert, Dave got up early to check out *Something*'s vital signs.

In addition to checking on the oil and water twice a day, Dave also lubricated suspension members, the water pump, and universal joints with a "sticky" type of oil that didn't tend to drip onto the ground but instead stayed around for a while.

We discovered, quite by accident, that nearby Ohio City was the site not only America's first automobile manufacturing plant, but also the first known automobile accident. Dave (right) and I pose next to a sign honoring John Lambert's dual achievements here in 1891.

We'd had a consistent, though minor, water leak out of the water-pump shaft, which Dave had been chasing daily without much success. Every morning he would carefully tighten the brass bushing at the front of the pump, being careful not to overtighten and damage it. On our third day, he repacked it with seal-packing material, which seemed to help somewhat. We initially thought the pump only dripped a little when the engine was shut off, but the windshield on Michael's Escape was usually coated with a fine, dirty spray at the end of each day, which led us to believe that it leaked all the time.

But Dave wasn't concerned with the water leak this morning—it was an oil leak that had his attention. Oil was leaking from somewhere (everywhere?) in the drivetrain and onto the hotel's fresh, immaculate pavement. He removed the floorboards and inspected the transmission for loose bolts, but they were all tight.

"There is no place in particular that the car is leaking from," Dave said. "I think it's just that we're running a constant 55 miles per hour, a speed much higher than the engine was designed to operate on, hour after hour. It's just seeping from everywhere."

I justified the oil leak as *Something* "marking its territory."

Thus far, Dave had added about two quarts of Shell Rotella oil, the lubricant of choice for cars of this era, to *Something*'s crankcase. "At this pace, we won't have to change the oil on this trip—we'll just keep adding and it will just change itself," he said.

Westward ho—Indiana beckoned.

ABOVE: A sight we saw a lot of on this trip; Dave had to constantly add oil and coolant because of *Something*'s habit of marking her territory wherever she went.

BELOW: For example . . . The largest puddles seemed to occur at the front door of hotels, on the newest piece of asphalt!

Central 2 Standard Time

Cozad, Nebraska, home of the official Lincoln Highway halfway point. The pavement change from asphalt to concrete under *Something* marks the point where we were an equal distance from New York City and San Francisco.

Once we got into the Midwest, especially in Indiana and Illinois, we occasionally had Lincoln Highway options. This leg, for instance, is from the original 1913 route, which was replaced by another route in 1928.

1. We gained a free hour! I love traveling east to west. It was about noon Eastern time, and like one of Pavlov's dogs, I began to salivate for lunch—but once we crossed into the Central Time Zone, I was no longer hungry.

As soon as we entered Indiana, we rolled off the modern Highway 30 and onto the original Lincoln Highway. The sign read "1913 Route." Even though today's Highway 30 runs parallel to the older route, sometimes as close as 100 yards away, the latter was a less rushed and more pleasant drive. I felt bad for the frantic commuters rushing by on the highway next to us.

As a bonus, we were able to travel through small towns that had been bypassed by the newer highways. I wish these places could talk—what an interesting story they could weave about life on the Lincoln Highway over the past 105 years. Perhaps they would tell us about the highs of the Roaring Twenties era, when buses filled with jazz musicians headed off to Chicago and other hot spots, or the lows of the Great Depression. Maybe they would remember Flathead V-8-powered Fords and big Chevy six-cylinders raced down the highway by adrenaline-fueled teenagers to impress their girlfriends, or those same teenagers shipping off to World War II, many never to return. A century of expectant mothers being driven to the hospital; newlywed couples heading off on their honeymoon; rural postal carriers delivering the mail through rain, sleet, and snow.

These towns would tell a story of increased traffic and prosperity for businesses during the Lincoln Highway's first seventy-five years or so—until the interstate highways went in, followed by large Walmart shopping centers that basically put many small downtowns out of business.

The story's ending may be a sad one, but at least we could imagine some of how things used to be as we drove our old car down the old route.

2. We decided to take the earlier Lincoln Highway route toward South Bend, Indiana. Highway 33 was an earlier Lincoln Highway route that was later bypassed to the south by the current Highway 30.

Our rationale to take the earlier route was twofold, First, Highway 33 was the more rural route, running two lanes all the way to South Bend; Highway 30 was certainly the straighter path across the state, but we longed to see the older Lincoln Highway landmarks. And two, Andy Beckman, archivist at the Studebaker Museum in South Bend, had offered to buy us a beer if we visited.

No brainer!

Fuel:
52.09 GALLONS
Distance:
837 MILES

3. "I walked the Lincoln Highway through Indiana twice," Jeff Blair, former president of the all-volunteer Indiana Lincoln Highway Association, told us over lunch.

"First I walked the original 1913 route in 2010—it is 171 miles and goes through all the small towns. There were no bypasses back then. The second time I walked, in 2013, was on the 1928 route to the south, which is 150 miles."

He prefers the original northern route to the "newer" 1928 version.

"The new route is just a straight line; there's not much more to see except farm fields and plains," he said.

Jeff and his staff are attempting to preserve the highway and the signage and buildings along it. His current project is trying to save a vintage auto dealership that could become a victim of the wrecking ball.

"It's along the Lincoln Highway and has such great old architecture," he said.

We met Jeff for lunch at Fashion Farm, a restaurant appropriately located along the Lincoln Highway in Ligonier, Indiana. It's a sleepy little town founded in 1835 and named after a British army officer, John Ligonier. Among Ligonier's claims to fame are its post office, which has reportedly been in continuous operation since 1848, and a synagogue that is one of the few built in the nineteenth century that are still standing.

Fashion Farm offers home cooking and amazing dessert. I polished off my Reuben with a slice of homemade rhubarb pie. Yum.

Jeff said he went through two to three pairs of New Balance sneakers during his cross-state walks. On his first trip, he walked with four people from his church, along with his wife.

Jeff Blair, past president of the Indiana Lincoln Highway Association, has walked across the state twice, once on the 1913 route, and again on the 1928 route.

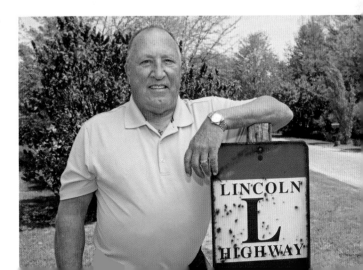

"None of us got blisters," he said.

The group of walkers sought to raise money for folks suffering from Alzheimer's disease.

"People would stop and donate money because they had heard about our cause. We donated $18,000 to Alzheimer's research," he said. "I also wanted to prove personally that, at sixty-three years old, I could still do something constructive.

"We stayed in hotels mostly, but a couple of nights we just stayed at our home. Unfortunately, we didn't lose any weight because people along the route fed us so well."

The toughest part? Finding bathrooms.

"On the first trip, two women joined us. The three guys could relieve ourselves behind the fifteen thousand trees along the way, but the poor women had to keep their eyes open for toilets."

On the second trip, Jeff walked by himself. "It was so boring," he said.

Even though we protested, Jeff wouldn't let us pay for lunch.

Nice guy.

4. Joyce Blue has lived along a brick-paved portion of the Lincoln Highway for most of her life.

"My dad bought this house when I was eight years old," she said. "I'm now sixty-eight. Our house, right over there, was once the site of the Noble County Post Office in 1832."

Joyce explained that her father, Graydon Blue, was once the town's pharmacist. He purchased this 80-acre farm to raise corn.

"The school bus used to pick me up right here," Joyce said, pointing to the red paving bricks that mark the original Lincoln Highway in front of her house. "These bricks are thick and as hard as a rock.

"These days the county maintains the road, so snowplows are tearing up the bricks. I'm afraid that one day they are going to just pave over it with asphalt."

Joyce moved away from the red-brick road for college, then lived in Fort Wayne and Chicago for a spell before moving back when her mom needed help.

"I had been working for Freddie Mac and traveled around the country for my job, but I always looked forward to coming back home."

5. Something started to get louder as we drove, and the car picked up an irritating metallic rattle that was triggered whenever we went over a bump. We pulled into a parking lot and Dave investigated.

It turned out that the weld holding the baffle in the exhaust pipe was broken. "It's getting ready to fall out, and if it does, the noise will be so loud we won't be able to stand it," Dave said. "We need to get it welded."

We started to search for a friendly looking repair shop that might do us a favor and allow us to borrow their welder. Soon we came upon a towing company, Campbell's Garage, also in Ligonier, and headed over. I asked if they had welding equipment.

It was a silly question.

"My father opened this shop in 1957, and all he had was a 1940 Ford sedan, a bad welder, and a toolbox," said Dan Campbell, who runs the business these days. "Eventually he built it into a salvage yard, repair shop, and towing business."

Dan proudly showed us his fleet of tow trucks, the largest weighing in at an amazing 96,000 pounds. This impressive vehicle has four rear axles and will deadlift 100 tons.

"The biggest thing we've lifted with that was a locomotive," he said. "When we had it built in 2001, it was the largest tow truck east of the Rockies." Dan said the truck cost $1 million when new.

He happily welded Something's exhaust baffle for us and wouldn't take a nickel for his labor. Then he and Dave spent some time looking at Dan's fleet of racing lawn mowers.

He also told us about the recent passing of his wife. "I bought a new Corvette," he said. "Sometimes I just feel like getting in it and driving and not coming back. It's so lonely here now."

Dan treated us, strangers, like family. It was just more of that Hoosier hospitality.

Thanks, Dan.

Dan Campbell to the rescue. When Something started making too much noise, we pulled into a towing and repair shop to have it fixed. Owner Campbell welded it and wouldn't take a penny!

6. Less than an hour after leaving Campbell's, we arrived at the Studebaker National Museum in South Bend. It was midafternoon, and as we pulled in, we discovered crews from four of South Bend's television stations, along with a small group of well-wishers, standing at the curb waiting for us. My friend Andy Beckman, the museum's archivist and the owner of a sweet four-speed, V-8, dual-exhaust Studebaker Lark, had arranged for a meet-and-greet in the parking lot.

Folks had been following our journey on our Facebook page and were eager to talk about it with us. Others, I suppose, showed up in hopes of a free beer. Regardless, everyone was eager to meet the crazy men who were willing to drive their semiopen car across the country through cold, heat, and rain.

Dave did his best to keep all the ladies in attendance satisfied by giving them rides in *Something*.

After a couple of hours, we all retired to Fiddler's Hearth, an Irish pub in downtown South Bend, where I enjoyed an amazing shepherd's pie and a tall glass of Guinness. A great way to end a pleasant day on the road.

Terry Meehan, who owns Fiddler's Hearth with his wife, Carol, approached me during dinner.

"I'm friends with a few of the local sheriffs, and they'd like to give you a police escort out of town in the morning, if you like," he said.

We had come into South Bend with four television crews waiting for us, and we'd be leaving in the morning with a police escort! Bring it on.

Suddenly we're stars! When we arrived at the Studebaker Museum in South Bend, Indiana, four television stations were waiting to interview us. This is me in the spotlight while in the background Dave is explaining the mechanical bits of our car to enthusiasts.

7. Ron DeWinter has seen South Bend in good times and in bad.

The seventy-two-year-old went to work at the Studebaker plant when he was eighteen, fresh out of high school. He followed the career path of his father, brother and brother-in-law.

"Studebaker offered the best-paying job in town," he said. "I started at $2.94 an hour installing headliners, which was about 10 cents more an hour than the average line worker made.

"It took three to four minutes to install a headliner. The station wagons were the most difficult. There were four or five of us, so I installed the headliner in every fourth or fifth car that came down the line."

Ron's tenure at Studebaker wouldn't last long, though—only three months. The plant closed down and Studebaker went out of business.

"The '64 Studebakers were nice cars, but they weren't selling. So the plant closed."

Today Ron has two Studebakers in his garage: a supercharged 1964 Studebaker R2 Hawk and a 1971 Avanti.

"Studebaker always tried to make their cars better," Ron said. "Look better and run better. They charged more for their cars because they paid their employees higher salaries and paid their shareholders higher dividends.

"Instead of high dividends, though, they probably should have reinvested in new products. For instance, the same V-8 engine was used from 1951 until 1964, so they didn't have to keep investing in new engine development. Management was not the best."

ABOVE: The Studebaker Museum staff and fans gathered around *Something* for a group shot before we departed for dinner downtown.

BELOW: Dave explaining how the pedals of a Model T function.

We had the number one parking spot in front of the Fiddler's Hearth in South Bend's City Center. Besides Guinness Stout and shepherd's pie, we had a great time with the Studebaker Museum staff and owner Terry Meehan.

Ron, who became a hairdresser after serving in the US Army, is a walking encyclopedia of Studebaker history.

"The company lost lots of money from 1954 to 1959, so President Eisenhower sent the company a big contract for airplane and truck engines. He refused to have Studebaker go out of business on his watch."

Even though Studebaker was the big industry in South Bend, there were other companies based there as well, including Bendix, Uniroyal, and Singer.

"When those companies left town, our tax base was hurt."

When Studebaker closed, Ron went to work in a restaurant, but then followed his older brother to barber school.

"He went off to Chicago and learned how to cut hair, so I did the same thing. I still cut hair and I love it. It gives me a chance to talk to people, which is what I love to do. My wife, Elizabeth, and I run the salon and have twenty employees."

Besides Ron's salon, South Bend's major employers today are the University of Notre Dame and Memorial Hospital.

"When I was a little kid, I was in love with my dad's 1953 Studebaker Starliner," Ron said. "I thought it was the best-looking car ever built. It was later called the Hawk.

"If the company hadn't gone out of business, I probably would have spent my career there."

STUDEBAKER

Even neophytes know that Detroit was the car-manufacturing capital of the United States, but there were other US cities where cars were produced that get little recognition. There was Buffalo, New York, for one, where the elegant Pierce-Arrow was produced. And Auburn, Indiana, where fabulous brands such as Auburn, Cord, and Duesenberg were manufactured.

South Bend, Indiana, is another. This factory town is where the Studebaker brand first produced wagons, then automobiles and trucks, from 1852 to 1967.

Two of the five Studebaker brothers, Clement and Henry Jr., had moved to South Bend in 1852 and became foundry men and blacksmiths. Initially they made metal components for wagons, but eventually they began building complete wagons. The brothers were perfectly poised to capitalize on the rapidly approaching era of horseless carriage vehicles, building both cars and wagons side by side until the automobile side became the more dominant business. The first automobiles the company produced were electric-powered cars in 1902, followed by gasoline-powered cars in 1904. Eventually a truck line was added when the horse-drawn wagon business declined.

By the 1920s, the company's business had grown to necessitate a 7.5-million-square-foot manufacturing facility located on 225 acres. The factory employed twenty-three thousand employees and produced 180,000 cars per year.

After the rationing of World War II, Studebaker was well prepared for the pent-up demand for new cars and featured some of the most stylish American cars ever made, including the Raymond Lowey–designed bullet-nose models, the Commander Starliner hardtop, and later the spectacular Avanti. What the company was not prepared for was the price wars initiated by Ford and GM to sell their products. When it became obvious that the company could no longer compete as an independent, Studebaker agreed to be acquired by Packard, a smaller but financially healthier manufacturer, in 1956.

The once-proud, but now nearly bankrupt South Bend company manufactured both Studebakers and Packards until 1962, when the Packard brand was dropped. Studebaker continued to be manufactured at both the South Bend and Hamilton, Ontario plants until the end of 1963, when South Bend was closed. The company ceased operations in 1967.

Designed by James Childs Architects—a firm local to South Bend—the Studebaker National Museum opened in October 2005. The Studebaker Corporation donated thirty-three vehicles to the City of South Bend in 1966, ranging from President and Conestoga wagons to examples of many of the automobiles and trucks produced by the company over six decades.

The museum is intended to be a fitting memorial to the men and women of the community whose vision, creativity, and energy built the products that are today our industrial manufacturing heritage, and to keep the flame of the Studebaker brand alive for generations to come. Its cars and displays are both attractive and interesting, and it is worth a visit, even for non–automotive enthusiasts.

8. A few weeks before setting out on this journey, I issued a call on Facebook asking for suggestions of points of interest and unique lodging opportunities along the Lincoln Highway. I was deluged with terrific places we could not miss, along with some great overnight accommodation ideas. Some folks offered us their spare bedrooms, and in one case a boarding house without plumbing.

Even though I considered every suggestion, some didn't work out—whether because they were too far off the Lincoln Highway or because we'd be passing through town at 11:00 a.m., far too early to call it a night.

But one option was so intriguing, I couldn't say no. I received a message from Dan Vandenheede. With their children out of the house, he and his wife, Jodie, kindly offered us the two bedrooms they typically rent out to travelers on Airbnb. But it was the next part of his message that especially got my attention.

"I also restore old VW campers and have a couple that you might want to consider staying in," he wrote.

I don't think I could ever receive a lodging invitation more appealing than Dan's. It didn't matter where Dave and Michael were going to sleep that night—this was my chance to connect with the inner hippie that has been lurking inside of me for the past half century.

Dan and Jodie live in Niles, Michigan, about 10 miles north of the Studebaker Museum in South Bend, Indiana. So after our museum meet and greet and our Irish dinner, we made our way north toward Niles.

Dan and Jodie made us feel like heroes by inviting a bunch of their car-crazy friends to a driveway party. Parked at their house when we drove up were a 1966 Mustang fastback, a 1967 VW convertible, and a 1972 VW bus with a Subaru engine conversion. Dan and Jodie, in addition to the two VW campers, own a VW convertible and a one-family-ownership, first-generation Mazda RX-7.

(A couple of months after our visit, when I called up Dan to clarify a couple of details about his campers, he told me that he and Jodie had just returned from a six-week vacation in Europe, where they'd added yet another vehicle to their collection. "We bought a 1990 non-synchro VW Westfalia camper that was equipped with a turbo diesel and a five-speed transmission," he said. "We fell in love with the diesel engine and its great

VW bus collectors Jodie (left) and Dan Vandenheede offered us lodging at their home in nearby Niles, Michigan. Even though Dave and Michael opted for the more traditional accommodations in the house, I was thinking seriously about the option behind Jodie's head . . .

gas mileage. Too bad it was never available in the States." When we spoke, the vehicle was sitting at the dock in Antwerp, Belgium. He was hoping it would soon be loaded on a freighter and be shipped to the States, where it could take up residence next to the couple's other two campers.)

But before sleep, there was a driveway party to attend! Dan and Jodie invited a few of their car friends over to celebrate our arrival into the South Bend area.

It was a great evening with great people who all wanted to know something about *Something* and our drive across the Lincoln Highway. If I weren't already a car person, I would sure want to become one so I could attend a party like that one.

When it started to get too dark to see our beer, Dan's and Jodie's friends started to leave and we started to make plans to get some rest. Not surprisingly, softies Dave and Michael chose the bedrooms in the house, but I was going for a camper. I had a choice of two: one a traditional VW "pop-up" and the other a late-model, tall-roof Adventurewagen.

I wrote up my notes from the day inside the Adventurewagen. It was built on a 1989 VW Synchro 4×4 platform that Dan and Jodie have driven as far away from Niles as Key West, Florida, and the Arctic Circle in Alaska. Dan bought it from the original owner in 2008 after several years of pestering him to sell. It had 38,000 miles on the odometer. Ten years later, when I stayed in it, that odometer read 90,000.

I'd never actually slept in a VW camper, but I have admired them from a distance my whole life. My mom, Johanna, is from Germany, so the only cars my parents ever drove when I was a kid were VW Beetles. In 1967, my parents almost bought a camper but chose a new VW Squareback instead.

So this was a first for me.

Lying there in the very adequate double bed, I had the sudden urge to light up a doobie and listen to Jerry Garcia. *Not that I would.* If I briefly considered it, it was only in order to give you, the reader, the full Woodstock experience.

Great place to stay, though. Even in the thunderstorm that was happening on the outside.

Good night . . .

9. In North Carolina, where I live, more than a few natives of the South have told me that the best place to sleep during a rainstorm is in a tin-roofed tobacco barn. Apparently the sound is intoxicating. I've never tried it,

THE VW ADVENTUREWAGEN

In 1963, Ed and Jereen Anderson had wanderlust, but a small budget. So they converted a Volkwagen Transporter van into a camper and hit the road, spending seventeen months visiting thirty-one countries on four continents. Their vehicle was transported by boat thirty-four times. Serious travelers.

When they returned to their California home, the couple set up a business to convert VWs into self-contained homes on wheels so other people could enjoy the same experiences they had. The original Adventure Camper company operated out of two locations, Sylmar in Los Angeles and Burlingame in northern California, and was in business from 1968 until 1973, when it went bankrupt. Insiders say that Ed became disillusioned with high-volume manufacturing and the complexities of setting up a nationwide network of dealerships and service centers.

In 1974, the Andersons reorganized and set up the Adventurewagen company, located near Fort Bragg in northern California. His idea was to establish a low-volume operation for a select customer base.

The company offered an alternative to VW's factory-offered Westfalia campers, featuring unique seating, cabinets, and storage options. The biggest difference between the Westfalia camper and the Adventurewagon conversion, though, was the tall, fixed fiberglass top that allowed adults to stand up in the center of the van. VW's own campers had a pop-up design, which had its advantages (that it could be parked in a standard garage) and disadvantages (that it didn't provide very good insulating and storage properties).

When Volkswagen ceased production of a suitable Vanagon model, Adventurewagen began to convert four-wheel-drive Ford vans into campers. Singer Jimmy Buffett apparently owns one of those.

It appears the Adventurewagen company continued to convert vans until 2002, when Ed simply closed the company in order to pursue his other hobbies and interests, most notably trail riding on horseback. He accomplished his dream of riding the Pacific Crest Trail from Canada to Mexico on horseback in 2012.

Ed Anderson died the next year, in 2013, at the age of seventy-seven. The lifelong adventurer suffered a heart attack while camping on horseback in rural California backcountry.

The vehicles he produced continue to be in demand today.

but now I feel like a fiberglass-roofed camper must be the next best thing.

At daybreak, I woke up and walked into Dan's and Jodie's kitchen to tell them I'd had the best night of sleep in my life! Fantastic.

We talked about VW campers while we ate some breakfast pastries, and Dan educated me about how he came to own his 1969 Sportsmobile, a VW van conversion from Anderson, Indiana.

"I bought it out of a junkyard on Beaver Island, off the coast of Charlevoix, Michigan, near the UP in Lake Michigan," Dan said. "It was in 1994. Cars were shipped to the island and used by residents, and when they died, they just stayed there in a small junkyard. The island is fourteen miles long and nine miles wide.

"So I got up there and bought the camper just before the crushers arrived."

One of Dan's friends who had partied with us in the driveway the night before was Jimmy Jaynes. Jimmy had brought the VW convertible, which he restored for his wife. He owns the Viking Grill, located just a few blocks away from my temporary VW residence. Dan recommended we go there for breakfast, saying that it couldn't be beat.

We followed his directions, which he said would take us right through true urban blight, before we arrived at the Viking Grill. He was right— lots of closed and rusted factories. It was a sad reminder of Niles's once-flourishing industrial past.

Jimmy is a busy guy. Not only does he run the restaurant and fix up old VWs, he is coaching his fifteen-year-old daughter, Shelby, to race cars on dirt tracks.

"Did you name her Shelby because of Carroll Shelby and his Mustangs and Cobras?" I asked.

"You bet," said Jimmy. "My kids are all named after cars: Stingray, Chevelle, Mercedes, and Shelby."

Oh, and Jimmy also plays in competitive pool tournaments. In fact, when he left Dan's driveway party, he went to play pool.

"I won," he said. "It's just what I do."

When my pancakes and bacon arrived at the table, I asked whether it was for two people. I was told it was a single portion.

So much for losing weight on this trip.

Dan's friend Jimmy Jaynes, who names his kids after cars, owns the Viking Grill, a great local dive that serves up amazing breakfast and lunch plates.

ABOVE: Fiddler's Hearth owner Terry Meehan arranged a police escort out of town. Corporal Randy Peppers (left) and Corporal Frank Hilbert, both from the St. Joseph County Sheriff's Department, agreed to escort our little car out of town during rush hour! Here they are giving Dave the instructions.

BELOW: Viking Grill pancakes are way too large for human consumption, but they were terrific, and I did my best to polish them off. Jimmy makes them square in shape to resemble a baseball diamond.

10.

After breakfast, we drove from Niles south back to South Bend for our appointed "police escort."

We were met in front of the Fiddler's Hearth by Corporal Randy Peppers and Corporal Frank Hilbert, both with the Saint Joseph County Sheriff's Department. So there we were in this little Model T with a sheriff's car in front of us and another behind, lights flashing and sirens blaring. It may have appeared to citizens that we were being run out of South Bend.

"Lock up your women and children! Them Model T boys are in town!"

When we came to a busy intersection, Corporal Peppers blocked all other traffic from coming through. We felt like royalty. Motorists pulled to the side of the road out of respect, probably thinking it was a funeral procession, but it was only a couple of guys in lowly yellow Model T.

When we got to the county line, our caravan stopped and we chatted with the sheriffs for a few minutes. They warned us of the Illinois boredom factor.

"If you need to drive an extra six hundred miles to avoid Illinois, do it," they told us.

Boy, tough crowd.

I told our two sheriff buddies that they had made our morning. Peppers and Hilbert said we had made their day, too. We all said goodbye and as they went back to work, we climbed into *Something* to continue our travel west. But just as we were about to pull back onto the road, a Dodge van pulled in front of us. Its occupants, Merle and Suzanne Miller of La Porte, Indiana, asked whether we were having trouble and if we needed any parts.

"I once restored a Model T and have a few parts in my garage—I think I have a set of fenders," said Marle. Obviously he felt sorry for our fenderless car.

They had seen us on the television news broadcast the previous night, so were familiar with our story. Suzanne told us that if we needed a place to stay in La Porte, we'd be welcome in their home.

11. My cell phone rang just as we were cruising through La Porte. It was a man named Stan Maddux, who was with WCOE radio and the Northwest Indiana *Times* and had seen us on the South Bend news the night before.

"I'd love to interview you," he said. "When will you be passing through La Porte?"

"As a matter of fact, we're passing through La Porte at this very minute," I told him.

So we pulled over at a gas station, and Stan quickly drove over to interview Dave and me as we sat in the car.

Fuel:
60.06 GALLONS
Distance:
1,113 MILES

We were within moments of leaving the state. It had been one heck of a nice visit, with nice scenery and neat people. Folks seemed to be resilient and optimistic—they live in the Rust Belt but are confident that "Things are turning around."

Indeed they are. These Hoosiers are OK with me.

I sincerely doubt that future travelers in driverless cars will have the opportunity to be interviewed by four TV stations, two newspapers, and one radio station; be hosted at a dinner in an Irish pub; sleep in a VW camper; have a police escort out of town; and meet strangers who'd offer up their spare Model T parts. I pity those poor future travelers.

12. Our drive through eastern Illinois was what you would expect from a Chicago suburb: miles of shopping centers and congestion.

As we continued west on the Lincoln Highway, the modern highway changed numbers from 30 to 31 to 38. We passed one congested Walmart shopping center after another. But eventually the congestion gave way to farmland.

We passed a "Seedling Mile" marker on Route 38 in Malta. I didn't know what that was, so I looked it up in my Lincoln Highway book.

When the Lincoln Highway was built, each state had Seedling Miles, which were the first paved mile of highway in each state. Some were paved in concrete, others in brick, but there was a strong push by the Lincoln Highway Association to have municipalities take pride and convert the highway from

Flashing lights and sirens in front and behind us meant we didn't have to stop for red lights or stop signs. We felt like royalty!

dirt, which quickly turned to mud with the slightest amount of precipitation. Cities and towns applied to construct Seedling Miles when the Lincoln Highway was first established. When a town was granted Seedling Mile status, it was the residents' responsibility to raise $2,000, which qualified them to receive two thousand barrels of concrete.

A little further west, we passed through the town of Rochelle and saw a mural of Emily Post. The scene commemorated her Lincoln Highway adventure on the side of a restored vintage gas station, now converted into a tourist office. There was no sign of any teacups. Outside of town were farm fields of rich, dark soil; having lived in North Carolina for more than three decades, I've seen way too much red mud, so this dark brown soil really got my attention. I wish I could have brought home just enough of it for our vegetable garden and flower beds.

Near the town of Ashton was a nostalgic section of Lincoln Highway, an unpaved gravel road that ran parallel to the railroad tracks, less than 20 feet away. Much of the original Lincoln Highway was built adjacent to railroad tracks, the highwaymen wisely deciding that the railroad builders had chosen the most efficient routes with the least amount of elevation changes. This piece of highway was particularly impressive because a freight train was sitting idle on our right side and rich farmland was on the left.

The wonderful rural scene was like something right out of a Johnny Cash song. Since there was no other traffic, we had some fun with

Once we were back on the Lincoln Highway, we were able to really open her up . . . or at least travel at 55 miles per hour. We bought the bicycle flag as an additional safety precaution to get the attention of other drivers.

Something, speeding and sliding on the dirt road along those railroad tracks like we were in *Bonnie and Clyde*.

Is it true that men are really just older boys?

We stopped in a little town called Franklin Grove, Illinois, for sunset photos during a time of day that Michael and other photographers call the magic hour. There was a sign at the Lincoln Highway National Headquarters building in Franklin Grove that instantly sobered us up: New York—999 miles, San Francisco—2,390 miles.

We still had quite a bit of driving to do.

In Dixon, Illinois, we passed a nice little house on a quaint street. It was the boyhood home of Ronald Reagan. Growing up in a wholesome hometown like this, it is easy to see how he was such a well-rounded person.

13. Except for the near-freezing temperatures we encountered in Pennsylvania, the weather had been nearly ideal on our trip so far. We'd had threats of rain now and then but only experienced light mist a few times while we were on the road. The only real rain had been during the night when *Something* was parked in the Vandenheedes' garage in Niles, Michigan, and I was sleeping in their VW camper.

Day 5 was a Chamber of Commerce day, with a big blue sky and temperatures in the 70s. Toward dusk, we crossed the Mississippi River and entered Clinton, Iowa.

TOP: A "Seedling Mile," a concrete mile of the Lincoln Highway, being installed in central Iowa. *Lincoln Highway Digital Image Collection, University of Michigan Library (Special Collections Library)*

ABOVE: We saw this tribute to Emily Post on a building in Rochelle, Illinois. It commemorates Post's 1915 drive along the Lincoln Highway, where she "almost" made it from coast to coast, with her son and her cousin.

We checked into a Hampton Inn for the night, not because we especially wanted to, but we couldn't find anything else suitable at dusk. Our plan was to drop off our luggage and find someplace cool to eat. When we walked into the lobby, though, it appeared as though we were walking into a party.

Adjacent to the check-in desk, in the area normally reserved for breakfast, a dozen or more people were eating, drinking, and making noise. And they had tunes, Tyrone Davis I think, on an iPhone sound system.

Dave wandered over to see what was going on while I checked us in, and Michael went through the nightly ritual of dragging his heavy camera gear out of the Escape, onto a luggage cart, and into the hotel room. It was probably 100 pounds of bulky gear from the car to the hotel room and back into the car again in the morning.

I once asked Michael why he just didn't keep the equipment locked in the car. He told me he used to, but one time his car was broken into in a hotel parking lot and he lost every piece of camera gear he owned. He said he'll never do that again.

So, when I finished checking us in, Dave came over and told us the partying people all worked for the same company and had invited us to have dinner with them. Such a deal!

It turns out that they worked with the US Army and spent lots of time in various places around the world, so when they check into a hotel, it becomes their home for a period of weeks. They even cook their own food on grills that most Hampton Inns offer out back. They were serving sausage, chicken, ribs, corn, salads, and coleslaw, and it was all terrific. Someone on their team was one heck of a cook, because they had marinated the meat all day before tossing it on the grill. Oh, and there was beer, too.

While most people were eating, drinking, partying, and talking, I sat next to a woman who looked as though she was in charge.

She was.

"We are civilian employees of the US Army and we do environmental cleanup," said Laura Graham, who was the project manager on this program. "We're getting rid of chemical weapons left over from the World War I era. We're working over at the Savanna Army Depot, which is nearby, right along the Mississippi River."

Laura told me that after the war, these chemical agents were shipped by rail to seven or eight depositories around the country, and the Savanna site was one of them.

"I'm talking in terms of millions of munitions," she said. "We neutralize the chemicals on site, so all that is left is scrap metal."

The crew wears special suits, similar to space suits, with gloves, boots, and masks. They also have a blast chamber where they blow up armaments in an explosive destruction system.

Obviously, with a job this stressful, this crew liked to let its collective hair down in the evening. Laura told me that they once had to neutralize chemical weapons off the coast of Syria. They outfitted a retired cargo ship and did all their explosions inside the ship while it was out on the water.

I bet they really partied hard on those nights.

ABOVE: Laura Graham was in charge of the disarmament crew below. She told me that many of the chemical weapons they were disposing of at the former Savannah Army Depot along the Mississippi River were left over from World War I.

BELOW: When we walked into the Hampton Inn, we walked into a party! Employees of a company that disarms chemical weapons had cooked up some amazing dinner items and invited us to join them.

. . . .

14. The town of Clinton, where we spent the night, is just a few miles north of LeClaire, Iowa. Do you have any idea what is headquartered in LeClaire? I sure didn't.

But our partying friends had told us we couldn't miss visiting Antique Archeology, better known as the store from *American Pickers*. You know—the show on the History Channel where Danielle Colby hangs out while Mike Wolfe and Frank Fritz travel around the country dragging in everything from old motorcycles to army helmets to road signs.

Fuel:
66.73 GALLONS
Distance:
1,220 MILES
. . . .

Much of that merchandise winds up here, in LeClaire. Some of it is for sale and some of it on display.

We had to visit.

We pulled *Something* into the parking lot, where we seemed to fit right in next to the 1950 Nash Statesman sedan that acts as the billboard for *American Pickers* World Headquarters. The business is one block west of Main Street and two blocks from the Mississippi River.

American Pickers might be the best thing that's happened to LeClaire in a long time. This pretty little burg on the banks of the Mississippi has become a tourist destination for both pickers and *Pickers* enthusiasts.

Two neatly restored vintage-type buildings make up the enclave. I found it interesting, though, that when I walked into the store I was bombarded with *new* merchandise, not rusty relics—I expected to see old dolls and carburetors and penny arcade games but instead saw new T-shirts and hats and coffee mugs. Old bits were scattered about, mostly as design elements, and either displayed a tag reading NFS (not for sale) or a number that was grossly overpriced.

It's funny, sad, and revealing that a show that is totally about the possibilities of finding rusty stuff sells new sweatshirts made from 100 percent cotton and Mike Wolfe–designed, artificially fatigued leather jackets in their retail outlet. Long live the entrepreneurial American spirit!

I spoke to a few folks who were shopping at Antique Archeology and milling about in the parking lot. One interesting fellow was Christopher Woodsum, from Olympia, Washington. He was driving a 1964 Studebaker Wagonaire station wagon, built, he said, one month before the Studebaker company went out of business. Funny, I wonder if Ron DeWinter, the former Studebaker employee we met in South Bend, installed the headliner in Woodsum's wagon? The timing would have been spot on.

Woodsum had left Olympia on April Fools' Day, about five weeks earlier, pulling a utility trailer that he had converted over one weekend into a camper. The trailer contained one single cot, a tiny refrigerator, and a camp-type stove.

AMERICAN PICKERS

Pickers Mike Wolfe and Frank Fritz have been searching through basements, attics, garages, and barns looking for trash and treasures since 2010.

The pair travel the country in a van and negotiate the purchase of motorcycles, car parts, gas pumps, signs, bicycles, toys and anything else that gets their attention. Then they collect or resell that merchandise at either their "headquarters" in LeClaire, Iowa, or their new outlet in Nashville, Tennessee. Fritz also sells merchandise at his own store, Frank Fritz Finds, in Savannah, Illinois, not far from LeClaire. The premiere episode of A*merican Pickers* aired on January 18, 2010, to 3.1 million viewers, the largest audience for a new show on the History Channel since *Ice Road Truckers* in 2007. The September 10, 2010, program entitled "Laurel and Hardy" garnered 5.3 million viewers in the twenty-five- to fifty-four-year-old age group, making it the number-one nonfiction program among that age group that year.

Wolfe, who owned a couple of bicycle repair shops earlier in his life, has been picking professionally for at least twenty years, much of that time operating under the radar. His cover was blown, though, when the concept he had pitched to a number of TV production companies was finally accepted. As the founder of the successful *American Pickers* concept, he has since diversified into a number of other businesses, including a signature clothing line, furniture design, and even record producing.

As the supporting cast member of the Odd Couple of Junk, Fritz seems to be the less aggressive but probably more likeable picker partner. He spent a long time as a fire-safety inspector but always enjoyed junk collecting and picking, so he jumped at the opportunity to join his boyhood friend, Wolfe, as a partner in the series. He has no business ambitions beyond his one outlet and said in a 2016 interview with the *Columbus Dispatch* that he will sell it all and just go back to being "Frank" when the show ends.

Even show hottie Danielle Colby is apparently a serious picker. When not guiding the boys to their next location, she searches for vintage costumes from the early 1900s.

Being a motorcycle enthusiast, his itinerary included visiting the motorcycle museum at Barber Motorsports Park near Birmingham, Alabama; seeing the sights at the Atlanta Motorama; driving to Cape Cod and seeing the Red Sox play at Fenway Park; and stopping in Augusta, Maine, to pick up a vintage motorcycle engine from his cousin. The engine had belonged to Woodsum's grandfather, and he was eager to find out what it belonged to.

He stopped at Antique Archeology to see if Mike Wolfe, also a motorcycle enthusiast, could help him identify the brand of the engine. But unfortunately Mike was out of town today, no doubt picking through more barns.

"I'm pursuing my bucket list in my 1964 Studebaker," Woodsum told me. He had driven 7,200 miles so far, including one 600-mile day across Vermont and New Hampshire. He told us his Lark station wagon was powered by an Avanti R1 engine that he installed for added horsepower.

Woodsum didn't travel lightly. Besides the motorcycle engine in his fully equipped trailer, he had a motor scooter, a canoe, and, believe it or not, an herb garden.

I've never seen anything like it. Lark station wagons have a partially retractable roof over the rear cargo area, so in nice weather he opened the roof to expose his plants to the sunlight as he drove down the road.

"I've been planning this trip for about a year," he said, almost too excited to get the words out of his mouth. "Ever since I retired from the public school system in my town. I figure I'll be home in about one more week."

Since Mike Wolfe was away, Woodsum was the most excitable person we met in LeClaire!

He wasn't the only person I talked to, however. I met a woman from Texas who had been living in Turkey since she and her husband were assigned there as part of the US Diplomatic Corps. She was an *American Pickers* fan who never misses the show and just had to stop here while on vacation. From Turkey!

Another couple, from British Columbia, Canada, made a point to visit *Pickers* world headquarters during their vacation in the US as well.

I was shocked that the program attracted such an international audience. If you had any doubt about the popularity of this TV show, look no further than the license plates on the cars parked at their retail outlet.

. . . .

15. Heading north and west out of LeClaire, we were set to catch up to the Lincoln Highway again about 20 miles west of Clinton. We drove through farm country on billiard-table-smooth roads. By now Dave and I were used to the strong, organic smells of Midwest farms and no longer looked at each other suspiciously.

We steered *Something* toward Colo, Iowa, which I had read was a classic crossroads town that offered the three essentials for life: food, fuel. and lodging. Fuel was our most vital essential—about every three hours we would frantically look for a gas station, specifically a Shell station because the company had kindly offered to pay for some of our fuel on this trip. (Shell is a partner in the *Barn Find Hunter* YouTube series I host for Hagerty Insurance.)

On our way to Colo, we stopped in an idyllic little town called Tipton around lunchtime. Tipton is not on the Lincoln Highway—we were still commuting back in to Highway 30—but it seemed like a nice place to stop for lunch. It is the county seat of Cedar County, Iowa, and 3,221 people live in the eastern Iowa town, according to the 2010 census. That census also revealed that 97.9 percent of the inhabitants are white and that Hispanic residents make up the second-largest category of citizens at 1.4 percent. Tipton was founded in 1840 and named after General John Tipton.

OPPOSITE TOP LEFT: One of the characters we met at Antique Archeology, the *American Pickers* World Headquarters in La Claire, Iowa, was Christopher Woodsum of Olympia, Washington. Woodsum had his grandfather's old motorcycle engine, and wanted to see if show host Mike Wolfe could help him identify it. Unfortunately Wolfe was on the road.

OPPOSITE TOP RIGHT: Woodsum was traveling around the United States for two months in this 1964 Studebaker station wagon, complete with a homemade camper trailer and a natural herb garden in the back of the wagon.

OPPOSITE BOTTOM: *Something* looked right at home in front of Antique Archeology's headquarters and next to their Nash billboard. Folks from all over the United States, and many from foreign countries, travel to the remote Iowa town to buy T-shirts and hats.

There's not much more that can be said about the place, and not much to do except eat, which is why we were there in the first place. The town's Facebook page features reviews on several of its restaurants and nothing in the upcoming events calendar. Oh, and two of the town's posted attractions include Tipton Adaptive Daycare and the Prairie Hills Retirement and Assisted Living Center. Now that sounds like fun!

It may not seem like I enjoyed Tipton, but I did. It was clean and honest, and it had a pretty downtown. Now we just had to decide where to eat.

We were literally approached as we exited the car by a Pizza Hut employee asking us to give their restaurant a try, offering us discount coupons for their lunch buffet. But, sorry, we didn't travel this far into the heart of America to eat franchise pizza. We chose the Tipton Family Restaurant instead. It stood on a corner right in the middle of town.

It was a Friday, so the restaurant's daily special was fish: catfish, flounder, or grouper. All three of us ordered grouper. Our server said fish was the traditional Friday meal in Iowa. When our plates were delivered there was a heaping portion of corn as the vegetable.

"That's the traditional Friday vegetable in Iowa," the server said.

It was a nice lunch, and I finished mine off with a piece of homemade blueberry pie.

Fish and corn: it's what you eat in Iowa on Fridays. We learned that lesson at the Tipton Family Restaurant in Tipton, Iowa, over lunch. We polished off the terrific grouper meal, then had a piece of homemade pie for desert.

16. "Excuse me, sir, would you please hand me my hat?" Dave asked a man who was pumping gas into his car next to ours.

We had just fueled up after a few hours of driving across the Iowa landscape. When we finally stopped after a long time without seeing a gas station, we darted toward the first general store we saw that had gas pumps. We had just finished pumping 10.8 gallons into our 10-gallon tank—yes, we had been nearly dry—and both of us had just climbed back into *Something* through the right-side door and were all buckled up when Dave's hat blew off.

That meant I, as the passenger, would have to unbuckle and maneuver my way out the tiny passenger door to retrieve it. That's when Dave had the idea to ask the fellow to pick it up for him.

"Sure, here you go, sir," said the man.

As we pulled away, I wondered if he thought we were just lazy. In fairness, we were, but also tired.

What folks didn't realize is that with Dave being more than 6 feet tall, and me at almost 6 feet 3 inches, climbing in and out of that little door was no easy task. Also, even though

Something had both driver-side and passenger doors, we both had to enter and exit out of the passenger door because the driver's door is blocked by the steering wheel and the emergency brake lever, making it nonfunctional except for children.

17. The general store where we refueled was in Tama, Iowa, home to one of the most iconic symbols of the Lincoln Highway's 3,400-mile span. The Lincoln Highway Bridge, with the highway's name emblazoned in the concrete guardrails, was built in 1915 as a way to promote the nation's first cross-country road. It spanned a small creek.

Fuel:
77.53 GALLONS
Distance:
1,415 MILES

Even though the Lincoln Highway bypassed Tama in 1926, the bridge endures as one of the highway's most famous landmarks.

The guardrail signs make it an ideal, but perilous, photo op. The road has lots of traffic, so photographers and spectators on the narrow bridge take their lives into their own hands to shoot a selfie.

In 1976, the bridge was listed in the National Register of Historic Places, and private donations were secured to restore the bridge in 1987. A plaque next to it reads, "It stands as a dramatic reminder of a time when few roads were paved and the campaign to 'Get Out of the Mud' had just begun."

18. We drove past freshly plowed fields with soil just moist enough that dust wasn't flying, but dry enough that the tractors' tiller blades weren't getting clogged. We drove past farmers who were plowing beautiful, geometric designs into their wonderfully rich soil.

I grew up on Long Island, where the soil is basically sand. And my adopted home is North Carolina, which is famous for its red clay. So it was instant jealousy when we drove past these plowed fields of dark chocolate soil.

In the middle of this farm country I saw signs that puzzled me. They had a symbol of a wind turbine with a red circle around it and a diagonal line through it. Words below the image read, "Keep our Skies Clear." In other words, these people didn't want wind turbines in their backyards.

What was I missing?

One of the signs was, ironically, placed on the front yard of a home where wind turbines could be seen innocently spinning off in the distance on one side, and a nuclear power plant was spewing out steam on the other side.

Do these folks prefer a potentially lethal atomic energy station next door, or perhaps a nice coal plant spewing black smoke out of tall chimneys?

I'll get off my soapbox now.

19.

When we made it to the restored crossroad town of Colo, Iowa, I instantly fell in love.

I had called to reserve a couple of hotel rooms earlier in the day, speaking with Sandy Huemann-Kelly. She had seemed hurried and out of breath, and I would realize why when we checked in. In addition to the hotel in Colo, Sandy also runs the local restaurant, which—along with the adjoining gas station—has been a Lincoln Highway landmark since 1923. She is the caretaker of the town's historic preservation efforts.

Arriving in Colo, at a place called the Reed-Niland corner, I discovered the gas station, restaurant, and hotel actually sit at a significant crossroads: the intersection of the Lincoln Highway and the Jefferson Highway.

Call me ignorant, but I hadn't heard of the Jefferson Highway before. As it turns out, it is the historic north–south equivalent of the Lincoln Highway that connects Winnipeg, Manitoba, Canada, with New Orleans. It is named in honor of Thomas Jefferson, for his role in the Louisiana Purchase.

Sandy was a school teacher and librarian in Virginia for thirty years before she and her husband decided to return to their native Iowa. They both became involved as volunteers in the Lincoln Highway Association.

"It was December 2010, and we were visiting from Virginia over Christmas," she said. "The [Lincoln Highway] Association wanted this site open and operating for the highway's centennial.

ABOVE: *Something* speeding by one of the most iconic Lincoln Highway landmarks, the Lincoln Highway Bridge in Tama, Iowa. Ironically this bridge is no longer part of the current Lincoln Highway system, but it is one of the most photographed along the 3,000-plus mile route.

RIGHT: One of the most-photographed Lincoln Highway landmarks is this bridge, whose rails spell out the name of the highway. The bridge was built in 1915 and is still in use today. *Library of Congress*

They were looking for someone to operate the café and hotel, which had been restored between 2003 and 2008."

Well, by the time the holidays were over, association members had Sandy convinced that she was the one to run the place.

"It had been closed for about a year and a half when I took it over. I had to do a little bit of painting, but the buildings had been restored with funding grants and matching grants just a couple of years earlier."

Sandy, who has operated the businesses since 2011, could not have imagined hotel and restaurant management would one day be included on her resume.

"I would have zero interest in running a café except this one," she said. Clearly her educational experience can be put to good use at this property—she is working in a living museum.

"I have school groups come through here. I meet interesting people and I'm able to keep on learning."

But Sandy is as busy as a one-armed paper hanger. When I called about lunchtime the day before, she was probably serving people at the lunch counter or busing tables.

"I had to learn everything about the business," she said. "And right now we're short staffed, so I'm working extra while also interviewing for new employees."

Besides busing and serving, Sandy also does some cooking, takes payments from diners, and cleans the hotel rooms. She has a pleasant and refreshing personality and does a good job fulfilling the role as a diplomat representing this historic site. But don't think her library upbringing means she is laid-back; she has a wild side as well.

"I once rode all the way from northern Iowa to Virginia and back for my sister's wedding in a sidecar connected to my husband's motorcycle. It rained for 900 of the 1,100 mile trip!"

She said old cars and car groups stop at her café and hotel all the time.

"We had a couple of Model As driving through when one blew a head gasket," she told us. "They changed it right out there in the parking lot."

For a while that evening we parked *Something* in front of the old Reed gas station. As it was getting dark, the lights at the station made for a spectacular backdrop. Michael had his camera on a tripod and was shooting in the low light with a very slow shutter speed.

People who live in Colo started to come over and see what was going on, so we met some of Sandy's neighbors. Joseph Shircliff brought his nineteen-month-old son, Bubba, over to see our old car.

One of the places I'd been looking forward to visiting, the Colo Hotel at the Reed-Niland Corner in Colo, Iowa. This operating hotel and restaurant, along with the adjacent restored gas station, are an accurate reminder of what greeted travelers during the early days of the Lincoln Highway.

"He loves everything with a steering wheel," Joseph told us. Bubba certainly enjoyed his time in the driver's seat of *Something*.

20. We arrived in Colo, Iowa, at 6:30 in the evening and departed at 8:30 the next morning. During those fourteen hours, we had dinner, slept eight hours, ate breakfast, and purchased gas.

We also became integrated into the Colo community, however briefly. Sandy introduced us to volunteers who staff the old gas station, historians, and neighbors. Seeing our Model T, folks came over and introduced themselves and their children to us. These Iowans have amazing amounts of civic pride. They are proud of their communities, their jobs, and their families.

This had been my personal favorite stop of the trip so far. I'm so glad we were able to spend the time we did.

Just before we departed Colo, Sandy stuck her head out of the café door and warned us of the Nebraska wind.

"It's constant and it comes out of everywhere," she said.

Thank you, Sandy. Nice meeting you.

21. We had been communicating with a gentleman named Mark Anderson through our Ford Model T Coast to Coast Facebook

REED-NILAND CORNER

The tiny town of Colo, Iowa, was incorporated in 1876, the year of our country's centennial. According to the most recent census, only 876 people resided there in 2010.

Besides a small commercial district, it would be easy to pass through Colo in the blink of an eye, but you would miss one of the more significant landmarks along the Lincoln Highway. In 1923, Charles Reed built a small gas station, L & J Service, named for the initials of the Lincoln and Jefferson Highways, which intersected there. Besides selling fuel, Reed also repaired cars. Seeing an opportunity, his nephew's family, the Nilands, opened a café next door. The Nilands also built sleeping cabins that they rented to passing travelers.

The two families' businesses were prosperous into the 1960s, but when I-80 was completed and the Lincoln Highway was rerouted 5 miles south, the businesses could not survive. The gas station closed in 1967, followed by the restaurant and hotel in 1991.

A few years later, the city of Colo bought the properties with the intention of reviving them as operating historic landmarks. A work crew of both paid contractors and volunteers invested five years in the restoration.

In 2003, the restaurant and hotel both reopened as operating businesses. The adjacent gas station became a museum and is staffed by local volunteers.

page. (I'm pretty sure that bit of technology wasn't around when the Lincoln Highway was built, but it definitely helped our trip.) Mark told me he had a friend, a farmer named Darrell Crouse, who also owned a Rajo-powered Model T speedster. He said that Darrell would like to see ours and asked if we'd like to stop over.

To sweeten the pot, Mark told me that Darrell also had buildings full of old cars and tractors.

Well, Darrell lived right off the Lincoln Highway in the town of Boone, Iowa, not far from where we were. And he seemed like the kind of guy we'd like to meet.

Boone was originally called Montana when it was founded in 1865, but the name was changed six years later. Because a rail line ran through town and numerous coal veins run throughout the region, coal mining became the dominant industry in Boone.

Former First Lady Mamie Geneva Doud Eisenhower was born at the house on the corner of Carroll Street and Seventh Avenue, also known as the Lincoln Highway, in 1896. The first Casey's General Store, a regional chain where we purchased both fuel and refreshments on this trip, opened in Boone in 1967.

The town was to be the site of a huge bronze statue of Theodore Roosevelt, standing eight times the president's actual size. But the statue was commissioned in 1941, during World War II, and the 4,000 pounds of bronze that was required for the statue was claimed by the war effort. So in 1946, after

ABOVE LEFT: The lady who keeps all the balls in the air, Sandy Huemann-Kelly, who runs both the restaurant and the hotel. The former teacher and librarian considers it an honor to work in this living museum.

ABOVE RIGHT: You can call me Bubba. A neighbor to the hotel, Joseph Shircliff, brought his nineteen-month-old son across the street to see our car. Joseph said Bubba loves anything mechanical, meaning that one day he'll probably be a terrific farmer.

the war was concluded, a smaller version of the statue was produced and today sits on a granite foundation in the town's McHose Park.

We pulled into the Darrells' long driveway and up to the barn where his speedster was parked. Before I had a chance to meet either Darrell or Mark, I met Rosie, Darrell's amazing wife.

"See that Model A pickup?" she asked, pointing. "I bought that for one of Darrell's birthdays. Paid $300 for it. And that other Model A over there, we paid $150 for that one. We were so broke, I had to borrow the money."

As Mark and Darrell discussed the finer points of Model T speedsters, Rosie guided Michael and me through one of their large barns. She pointed out their Model T roadster, a 1956 Thunderbird, and a huge, *huge* steam engine built by Case. Darrell came in and told us about the Case.

"My father bought that in the early 1950s," he said. "We've owned it since then, but it hasn't been out of this barn in at least ten years. To move it is just too much work."

And there were so many vintage tractors—thirty that I counted in this one barn alone. I was drawn toward an attractive Moline Universal model, which Darrell said was built in 1915 or so. It was front-wheel drive and was powered by a two-cylinder, horizontally opposed engine.

"It's the oldest tractor I own," he said. "My father bought this one when I was in the fifth grade."

He also showed me his coral and white 1956 Ford Sunliner convertible. "I bought this in the 1960s," he said. "It was a California car."

Rosie prefers the Sunliner over the Thunderbird. "That T-bird is too tough to drive," she said. "Plus it only has two seats."

Darrell collected collections. He had too much of everything.

"Every now and then, when I'm rummaging through one of the barns I discover something I didn't know I had. I collect everything but old women, but now that I've been married this long, I have one of those, too!"

He and Rosie looked at each other and smiled. She had apparently heard that one a few times before.

Darrell inherited many of his tractors from his father, but he proudly pointed to one that was extra special.

"See that Allis-Chambers over there? I bought it brand new in 1954 when I started farming my 550 acres," he said. "Before that I'd use my father's tractor. Sometimes friends and I go to tractor rides with it where five hundred tractors will show up and just ride down the road for three days. Women don't go because it would be too uncomfortable for three days." Plus there's only one seat.

Rosie told me that these tractors haul wagons behind them, which provide a place where the farmers can sleep. Then there is a chuck wagon that cooks and serves food. And, thankfully, there is a shower wagon.

I imagine these tractor rides must resemble an agricultural version of the Hells Angels.

Darrell told us he has an airplane hangar where he used to keep a J-2 Piper Cub and a Steerman, but he sold the planes long ago, and now it's just filled with junk. Rosie piped up when she heard her husband discuss the airplanes.

"There were times I'd be planting out in the field, and here would come old Darrell flying over, waving and just having a good time. He knew how to get out of work."

As we were walking out of the main barn, I noticed a car that resembled one I have in my own garage at home: an old VW convertible. Darrell said his is a 1958, but it looked identical in color to my 1960 convertible.

"I started to restore it, but I've given up," he said. "I've installed new floor boards, but it's too hard for me to finish, so I just need to sell it as is."

For about ten seconds, I thought about making Darrell an offer for the car—but quickly came to my senses when I realized that I hadn't driven my own VW in fifteen years. Why on earth did I need another one? (Or at least that's what my wife would ask.)

We had to get back on the road, but Darrell and Rosie kept insisting that we look in some more of their barns.

This huge steam engine still sits on Darrell's tractor barn today. This photo was taken soon after this father purchased it in the early 1950s. Darrell and his father are both sitting in the back of the engine, his father is on the left, Darrell is second-to-left. *Crouse family collection*

"OK, one more," I said. "But we've got a lot of miles to put under our belt today. We're trying to average 250 miles a day, and at 55 miles per hour, that's a long day."

They guided us into another barn toward the front of the property; Darrell pulled open the door and it was absolutely crammed with stuff. *American Pickers* would be in their glory.

My eyes went immediately toward the old motorcycle sitting in the center of the crowded floor.

"My father bought this Harley Davidson for me brand new in 1948," Darrell said as he proudly showed us the bike. "I was sixteen years old. My brother and my dad each had one too. This one is an FL74 Panhead.

"In 1949, I was riding it when a car hit me. I had a compound fracture of my finger."

He showed me the finger, still crooked today.

"The car wound up on top of me, broke my finger and my wrist," he said. "It took a year for the dealership over in Ames [Iowa] to repair the bike."

Amazing that he still owns this Harley nearly seventy years later. Darrell said he still rides it, but not as much these days.

While we were looking at the cars, trucks, tractors, and motorcycle in the second barn, friends kept dropping over to tell Darrell and Rosie about the yard sales and garage sales they had visited that morning. Suddenly I felt bad that our visit had probably prevented this couple from participating in their weekly ritual.

Darrell pointed to another motorcycle, a two-wheel-drive two-wheeler called a Trail-Breaker. He said he had once been an area dealer for the brand. I remember seeing them in ads in *Popular Mechanics* magazine when I was a kid—as a young teenager, I always imagined how cool it would be to take off through the woods on that bike, going through fields and streams.

"They were made in Keene, New Hampshire, where I think they are still being built today," he said, "I became a dealer so I could buy a few for myself, my boys, and my friends at wholesale."

Darrell and Rosie had lots more barns and sheds, but we were running out of time.

"I have way too much stuff," Darrell said. "When I die, you should come to the sale."

At eighty-five years old, Darrell still

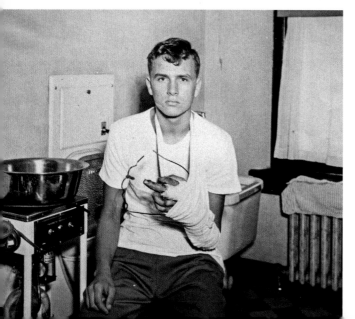

This is Darrell after a motorcycle accident in 1949. He still owns the Harley-Davidson his father bought him in 1948.

has way too much going on to talk about an estate sale. He is a lifelong farmer who has spent sixty-five years working his own fields.

"I've been farming since I was six or seven years old," he said. "That's when dad put me on a tractor for the first time. I grew beans, corn, oats, and hay on my farm; that's about it. And in the wintertime we would raise pigs. We'd buy them when they were just little piglets and we'd feed them all winter. When we sold them in the spring, in a matter of months they had grown to over two hundred pounds."

Darrell also had a custom feed grinder that other farmers in the area used to rent to grind their corn and oats.

"Anything to make a living," he said.

I asked Darrell if he had any children who might take over his farm one day.

"My daughter's husband rents our fields and farms it now. Between his own property and what he leases, he farms about 7,000 acres all together."

He is pleased that the farm he inherited from his father will be passed down to another generation in the family. His and Rosie's other daughter is a school teacher.

Darrell is sad about the fact that so many farmers' children have no interest in taking over their families' businesses.

"It's all I've ever wanted to be is a farmer," he said. "It was a free and friendly business. It used to be that we'd work side by side with our neighbors, and we'd stop and talk with them and we'd all get along. Neighbors are not doing that anymore. It's a whole new ball game today."

He told me that these days, when a farm goes up for sale, either a neighbor will buy it and add it to their farm or it will be sold to one of the big farming

ABOVE: Clobbered by a 1939 Ford in 1949. The wreck caused Darrell to break his finger and his wrist. Today, almost seventy years later, his finger is still bent, but the Harley looks as good as new!

FOLLOWING PAGES: Surrounded by dozens of tractors, Darrell Crouse (right), Rosie Crouse (center), and their friend Mark Henderson bid us farewell after an amazing visit to their farm in Boone, Iowa.

conglomerates. Darrell lives just 3 miles from where he grew up in Boone, so he knows the town just about better than anybody.

"It used to be a lot of fun to go to town," he said. "Downtown we had gift shops and a jewelry store, clothing stores, and three dairy stores where you could get ice cream. And we had three theaters, so we had a choice of movies on a Saturday afternoon."

That all changed when Walmart opened up on the other side of town.

"They really closed this town down when they moved in. Now we have to drive to Ames or Des Moines if we want to buy a nice pair of shoes.

"Rosie and I don't like to shop at Walmart, but anymore, this is the only place to go."

Darrell told me that when Walmart announced they'd be opening in town, some residents grumbled, but nobody was prepared for the negative effect the chain would have on the local businesses.

Rosie also grew up in Boone, but on the east side—across town from her future husband, who grew up on the west side.

"We were married in 1956, and I went to work for the telephone company," she said. "I worked there for twenty-two and a half years until they went to dial phones. I was laid off when they closed our office."

Rosie started off as a switchboard operator handling local calls. "Number, please," is what she said hundreds of times a day as she connected callers through a hundred wires in front of her. "There were only so many lines one girl could handle by herself. But those people didn't want to wait. If there was a big snow storm, all the lights on my switchboard would light up.

"I made $34.50 a week as a local operator. Then I advanced to being a long-distance operator. When I finally left the phone company as a supervisor, I was making $100 a week. Being a supervisor is the toughest job, because people would cuss me out, but I always had to be nice, whether I wanted to be or not."

One Boone family Rosie likely assisted many times as a young operator was the Douds. In 1916 at nineteen years old, the second child of John Doud and Elivera Carlson, Mamie, married an ambitious twenty-five-year-old Lt. Dwight D. Eisenhower. Mamie lived the life of an army wife as her husband eventually rose to the rank of five-star general. In 1953, he was elected the thirty-fourth president of United States, an office he would hold for two terms.

Even though Mamie's immediate family relocated to Denver, Colorado, the president and the first lady would visit her aunt and uncle in the little town of Boone.

"They would come to town about once a year when he was president," said Rosie. "His big black car would drive slowly down Main Street, and everyone knew the president was visiting.

"The Secret Service would take over all the town's telephone operations whenever he visited, just to make sure nothing funny was going on. I think I shook the president's hand once, but I certainly knew all the Secret Service agents."

Rosie said President Eisenhower once sent a photo to the girls in her office to show his appreciation for their service.

"It was a photo of him in his military uniform," she said. "It said he was appreciative of our efficient and loyal service, and [was] signed, 'Best Wishes, Dwight Eisenhower.' When the office closed, they threw out the photo, so I took it home and still have it today."

Before we departed from the Crouse farm, Darrell reached into his pocket and said he'd like to give each of us one of his nuts.

Since there were three of us, I thought that would be pretty talented.

He pulled out three buckeye tree nuts, which had come from a tree in their yard, and said that if we held onto them, they would bring us good luck.

"I've had one in my pocket for forty years, and look at me!"

Darrell and Rosie are some of the nicest people I have met in my life. They are authentic, humble, funny, and interesting, and they have experienced so much from their little corner of the world in Boone. They reminded me of a farm version of the comedy team George Burns and Gracie Allen—what an amazing couple! I could have stayed with the Crouses all day and listened to their stories.

I asked whether I could stop by and visit if I ever passed through the area again. They said they would love it.

Not more than I.

As we climbed back into *Something* to continue scooting down the road, Darrell gave us a piece of wisdom that we should all take to the grave with us: "All you get out of life is what you eat and the fun you had."

Amen, brother.

The photo of President Eisenhower that Rosie Crouse took with her the day her telephone office closed in 1978. It still sits on a shelf in her home today. *Crouse family collection*

22. It's interesting that Mamie's husband, Dwight D., figured into cross-country travel from the very beginning of his military career. As a young officer, he was part of a 1919 caravan of military vehicles

TRANSCONTINENTAL
MOTOR CONVOY

On July 7, 1919, a convoy also known as the Truck Train of the US Army Motor Transport Corps began a sixty-two-day, 3,251-mile journey from Washington, D.C., to San Francisco. It was the largest convoy of military vehicles ever assembled and was undertaken in the hopes of selling cities and states on the importance of building an interstate system of roadways.

An ambitious twenty-eight-year-old West Point graduate, Lt. Capt. Dwight D. Eisenhower, had been the officer in charge of tank training at Camp Colt near Gettysburg, Pennsylvania. He was becoming increasingly disillusioned with his military career, believing he was destined to become a paper pusher with nothing to show for a career desk job besides a big belly. So when the opportunity to command a cross-country caravan of vehicles arose, he volunteered right away. It was just the adventure he sought.

In all, manpower sent on the convoy included twenty-four officers, fifteen War Department observers (including Eisenhower), and 258 enlisted men. The eighty-one participating vehicles included nine motorcycles (Indian and Harley-Davidson); eleven passenger cars (Cadillacs, Whites, and Dodges); five ambulances (General Motors); and forty-six trucks (¾-ton Dodge delivery vans, 5-ton Macks, Whites, Packards, Rikers, and four-wheel-drives of various sizes). Two of the trucks carried spare parts, one contained a blacksmith shop, two were mobile machine shops, two 750-gallon tankers carried fuel, and another that carried water. Additionally, there were two ambulance trailers and four kitchen trailers.

One trailer called a Loder was actually a pontoon capable of floating across rivers. One Cadillac was fitted with a 3-million-candlepower searchlight. The largest vehicle was the $40,000 Militor, an "artillery wheeled tractor" with a wrecker winch that was capable of lifting and towing disabled vehicles out of trouble. The decision to bring this huge vehicle would quickly prove to be a wise one.

Setting off, the massive convoy circled Potomac Park, near the South Lawn of the White House. Reports state that roads from Washington D.C., through Nebraska were well made and solid, but once the caravan arrived in the West, the trucks began getting stuck in ditches, sand, and mud for hours at a time.

En route to California, the vehicles experienced 230 road "incidents," which included accidents, breakdowns, extrications, and vehicle adjustments. Nine vehicles had to be retired, unable to complete the trip. Twenty-one men were injured and could not complete the trip. The convoy also broke eighty-eight wooden bridges during the trip.

The Transcontinental Motor Convoy averaged less than 6 miles per hour and arrived in Oakland, California, seven days behind schedule. On one memorable day in Utah, the caravan traveled just 15 miles in seven and a half hours.

Despite all the complications, the trip did allow the military personnel to interact with residents of small towns across the entire country. In honor of their arrival, citizens often organized dances, concerts, chicken dinners, barbecues, and rodeos.

At the trip's conclusion, Eisenhower declared the expedition a success: "The officers of the Convoy were thoroughly convinced that all transcontinental highways should be constructed and maintained by the federal government. There was a great deal of sentiment on improving the highways."

that departed from the White House on July 7, destined for California. The caravan consisted of cars, motorcycles, trucks, ambulances, machine shops, and mobile kitchens.

Their destination: San Francisco. They averaged just 5 miles per hour, and the first Transcontinental Motor Convoy took two months to finish its journey.

Eisenhower never forgot his cross-country trek; thirty-six years later, on June 29, 1956, Eisenhower—by then the president—signed into law the Federal Aid Highway Act, which called for the establishment of controlled-access highways across the United States. As of 2013, nearly 48,000 miles of interstate highways had been built.

Even though three states all claim to have laid the first miles of interstate—Missouri, Kansas, and Pennsylvania—it was Missouri that was awarded the first interstate highway paving contract for Highway 40 (now Interstate 70) on August 2, 1956, just one month after the president signed the bill.

With the opening of I-70 through Glenwood Canyon, Colorado, in 1992, the Interstate Highway System was proclaimed to be complete. It had been estimated that it would cost $25 billion and take twelve years to create, but the system actually cost $114 billion over the thirty-five years it took to construct. That $114 billion, when adjusted for inflation, is equal to $1.2 trillion in today's dollars.

23. Iowa is a big state. It takes up two full pages in my 2008 Deluxe Roadmaster Atlas. My Lincoln Highway directory tells me that Iowa is 360 miles across, which is not the widest state by far; Nebraska, Wyoming, and Nevada are each more than 400 miles.

But driving through the state, Iowa just didn't seem that wide. Perhaps it was the scenery and elevation changes—there were beautiful farm fields and large wind-turbine farms to keep a motorist's attention and prevent boredom from setting in.

Iowa is one of those flyover states that few travelers from either coast would ever seek out as a hot vacation destination. We hear about Iowa every four years because of its position as a political battleground state in presidential primaries. News photos and TV broadcasts are filled with images of candidates eating homemade pie in down-home restaurants and holding babies at rallies. Then Iowa goes mostly silent for another four years as far as the rest of the country is concerned.

Lodging accommodations along the Lincoln Highway in Ames, Iowa. *Lincoln Highway Digital Image Collection, University of Michigan Library (Special Collections Library)*

I would love to visit this place again so I could see the sights that I didn't have time to see and meet people I wasn't able to meet. I think Americans who live on the two coasts take the Midwest for granted. We readily eat the area's beef, corn, and potatoes, but seldom do we consider the farmers who make those meals possible. Around here, you see bumper stickers on the backs of pickup trucks that read, "No Farmers, No Food." How true.

On this trip, I was fortunate enough to see many of those farmers driving their tractors in the fields early in the morning and well past sunset. More than a few times we saw headlights going back and forth across a dark farm field.

I was also fortunate enough to meet a few of them. Farmers work tirelessly to put food on tables of homes and restaurants of both coasts, everyplace in between, and outside the United States as well. Many areas have already laid claim to the catchy phrase, but the Midwest, specifically this Great Plains area, is truly the breadbasket of our nation.

Farmers work hard, but they play just as hard. They restore and collect tractors, ride motorcycles, fly airplanes, and build hot rods. And they love Model T Fords. Since Henry Ford was passionate about farmers, he built the Model T with them in mind.

And farmers live wholesome lives that we never have the opportunity to see firsthand when we fly over at 33,000 feet.

If you have a chance to take a slow road drive through Iowa, I hope you'll consider it. I certainly would love to make a return engagement.

24. Mark Anderson's ancestors arrived in Stratford, Iowa, in 1854 after a long journey from their native Sweden. They were a family of farmers who were drawn to the Midwest because of its abundance of flat, fertile soil. More than a century and a half later, Mark still carries on the family's farming legacy, although now on a part-time basis.

Mark has lived in Stratford his entire sixty-one years and never once considered leaving.

"My family has always lived here; I have no desire to live anywhere else," he said. "It's a slower pace, healthy lifestyle, and things are cheaper here than on the coasts."

Stratford has a population of about 725 residents, a number virtually unchanged since Mark was growing up there a half century ago.

"When I was younger, we had a busy little town here where everybody knew everybody. We had a movie theater, a couple of restaurants, and grocery stores. But these days most of those businesses have closed down. We still have an elementary school, but the town does not have enough students for our own high school, so we have to share one with a town about 20 miles away."

When he was growing up, it appeared that he'd remain in the agricultural business, but then the economy soured.

"I never went to college, although I always wished I had," he said. "Instead I went right into farming, working on a farm for a few years until I went to work for the local John Deere dealership for ten years. That was before the agricultural crisis hit around 1985. The prices of crops dropped, and interest rates were high."

Farmers could no longer afford to purchase new John Deere equipment, so Mark took a job driving a truck for a local grocery concern. Today, thirty-one years later, he's with the same company.

"I help a friend during the fall harvest with his 1,500 acres of corn and soybeans," Mark said. "His farm is considered small when compared to some of the others in the area, but he owns it all. He has one full-time employee and two of us part-time. I mostly drive a tractor or a combine, or a semitruck to the grain elevator. After harvest, we till the soil and prepare the ground for the next spring planting season."

Mark educated me about land leasing, which is when farmers expand the size of their land by leasing additional acres from neighbors. He told me that it is usually profitable for the landowner, but not so much for the tenant.

"Most ground leases go for $300 to $350 per acre or more per year, which can add up quickly. Plus the farmer still has to buy seed, fertilizer, and fuel, so it really cuts into profits."

I asked Mark about migrant farmers, and whether farmers in his area employ many of them. He surprised me when he said no.

"There are really no migrant workers here," he said. "If we grew more vegetables or fruit, we'd need that type of employee to pick crops, but we mostly use equipment to harvest what we grow here." He explained that what few migrant workers there are in his area tended to be employed in packing and processing plants.

Mark and his wife, Joan, who is one of ten children in her family, have been married for thirty-eight years. They have two daughters, one son, and three grandchildren—and they, too, are all content with living nearby.

ABOVE: We stopped at the Dairy Mart in Glidden, Iowa, for ice cream cones. We were greeted by Cierra Steinbach (right) and Meredith Grossman.

FOLLOWING PAGES: Darrell (right) and Rosie Crouse (center), with their friend Mark Henderson. Mark had been keeping track of our travels, and thought that perhaps, since the Lincoln Highway goes through their town of Boone, we might want to visit the Crouses and their collections.

25. We stopped in Glidden, Iowa, for lunch at the Dairy Mart, where we ordered burgers with fries and ice cream cones for dessert. And we had a good time talking with our servers, two Iowa girls named Cierra Steinbach and Meredith Grossman, about their futures.

Cierra had worked at Dairy Mart for five years and was a sophomore at the Des Moines Area Community College, where she was majoring in business. Meredith was a senior at Glidden High School and would be a freshman at the University of Northern Iowa in September.

On hot days, Cierra said she sells mostly ice cream, especially when the Dairy Mart features lemon, their favorite flavor. On cooler days, customers order more hot food.

"I have no idea what I want to do after school," Cierra said. "I'm only twenty—am I supposed to know by now?" That's the eternal question asked by every college student.

I asked her whether anybody famous ever came into the Dairy Mart.

"Well, the basketball players from Iowa State come in when they pass by," she said. "And Governor Terry Branstad used to come in until he came down with diabetes."

On the bulletin board next to the door were posted a couple of flyers for upcoming events, including such cultural events as a polka festival and a demolition derby.

Fuel:
85.42 GALLONS
Distance:
1,557 MILES
....

Just before we departed Iowa, we stopped in the town of Woodbine. This town has restored its red-brick-paved Main Street—part of the Lincoln Highway—to resemble the road surface when it was installed in 1921. Whether they were dirt, gravel, concrete or bricks, eventually all the roads of the Lincoln Highway were paved over with asphalt, but in 2003 the asphalt roads and concrete sidewalks in Woodbine were torn up and again resurfaced with 322,156 red bricks along the six-block downtown area. This section of road is now listed in the National Register of Historic Places.

Before crossing the Missouri River and into Nebraska, I'd just like to reinforce one more time how much we enjoyed traveling through Iowa.

26. Almost immediately after crossing the state line and into Nebraska, we started to take Sandy Huemann-Kelly's warning seriously.

"Man, that wind is something else," Dave said.

We were driving right into it. It wasn't strong enough to affect our speed—this motor was strong enough to push us through—but the car was working a little harder. I was certain that our gas mileage would suffer.

Something is an amazing car. As we approach the halfway mark on the Lincoln Highway, I think it's appropriate to pay honor to the vehicle that had gotten us this far without a moment's trouble.

The ninety-two-year-old Ford Model T had been an amazing and reliable friend. We'd had no mechanical issues to this point, and it's only because of our own ignorance that we ran out of fuel twice. Fortunately, both times we were within coasting distance from a gas pump. We had driven *Something* long and hard for as many as twelve hours a day and it never complained.

Dave had so far installed about 5 gallons of Rotella 15W-40 oil and probably one quart of Redline Shockproof lubricant on the valve tappets, universal joints, steering components, suspension, distributor drive, and rear wheel bearings.

This car is an amazing testament to the engineering genius of Henry Ford and the team of engineers who developed the Model T in 1908, and who continuously refined it through the end of its nineteen-year production run. Even though Ford was frugal and optimistic, I'm sure even he would be surprised to learn that *Something* was still operating with the same poured Babbitt bearings that his workmen installed almost one hundred years ago. It makes me wonder: how many of the econoboxes and SUVs we're driving today will still be operating in the year 2118? No matter the answer, I'll bet that *Something* will still be on the road then too.

27.
Driving through rural Midwestern towns, it was a treat to see vintage art deco designs on buildings. We passed many gas stations and other structures that featured corners of rounded glass and ceramic tile surfaces. Most of the stations were no longer pumping fuel and have, instead, been converted into visitor centers, boutiques, and cafés—or simply left to the elements.

These buildings were built to last. Made of sturdy cinderblock, they were constructed during an era when the quality of the product sold inside was judged by the quality of the structure on the outside. Oil companies didn't *need* to invest the extra dollars in the designs and quality construction of their buildings, but they *wanted* to make that investment. Those buildings represented the company's brand, and they wore it proudly. People who worked there felt proud, and the folks who shopped there felt good about the goods they purchased and remained loyal.

I look at the tin and sheet-metal gas stations of today, which can be assembled in days like a giant garden shed, and wonder how many will be standing five, six, or seven decades in the future—and how many will be converted into boutiques and cafés. Probably not many, because these buildings have short life spans. Investing in quality has become a thing of the past, companies sadly preferring to funnel more of the profits to their shareholders rather than investing in their future.

A trip to the gas station decades ago meant having your fuel pumped by a uniformed attendant. And while the fuel—which had snappy names like Good

FORD MODEL T: ONE OF THE MOST MAGNIFICENT MACHINES EVER BUILT

When a group of motoring journalists decided in 1999 to collaborate on determining the century's most significant automobile, their list of candidates started with one hundred vehicles. That list was winnowed down to twenty-five, and by the end, the Model T Ford was decided as the winner hands down. Making this even more noteworthy is that most of the voting journalists were from outside the United States.

Who could have imagined when Henry Ford began producing the humble Model T in 1908 that this simple car would still be celebrated more than a century later? It finished well ahead of other finalists, all milestone vehicles as well, including the Austin Mini, Citroën DS, Volkswagen Beetle, and Porsche 911.

From its humble beginnings, the Model T was designed as a "universal car," one that could be modified to plow farm fields during the week and still take the family for rides in the country on Sundays. Besides plowing, Ts were used for endeavors such as sawing wood, pumping water, powering grain elevators, running shears, generating electricity, and even as snowmobiles. At least five thousand gadgets were developed, marketed, and sold through dealerships, catalogues, and even hardware stores and pharmacies that made the car either more functional or more attractive.

A total of 15,458,781 Model Ts were manufactured from 1908 until production was ceased in 1927 to make way for the more modern Model A. During those years, at least 2,200 other car brands surfaced and failed. Model Ts gave Americans mobility that they never had before. Able to navigate through mud and snow, motorists were no longer limited to traveling as far as a horse and buggy would take them. Cars allowed a freedom and a feeling of independence. They gave drivers the "ability to go where and when," free of schedules, as a *Harper's Weekly* story put it.

In 1907, a motorist noted that prior to the Model T, his travel had been limited to 10 to 12 miles from home so his horses would not would not be injured during the round trip. The automobile had given him the ability to travel 50 to 60 miles away in the same amount of time.

Henry Ford kept his cars purposely simple so that men and women could drive and repair the cars on their own with the minimum of fuss. The cars were easy to fix, parts were inexpensive, and they were cheap to operate. But Mr. Ford's simplicity didn't come easily or cheaply—critical parts were made of high-strength vanadium steel, which allowed components to be made smaller and lighter in weight but was expensive to produce.

Development of components such as crankshafts included experimenting with examples that were ¼ inch smaller in diameter from the standard crankshaft. When that size was proven to be too flexible, Ford was satisfied with his original design, knowing that he had developed the smallest, lightest component that was still functional.

"The less complex an article, the easier it is to make, the cheaper it is to make, and therefore a greater number may be sold," Ford once said. "The most beautiful things in the world are those from which all excess weight has been eliminated."

Every time efficiencies such as vanadium steel or his famous assembly line were developed, instead of increasing his personal profits, Ford would reduce the retail price of the car. From an original price of $800, the Model T gradually came down to $520, and ultimately to $295 near the end of its life in 1926. This at a time when other car companies charged ten times that and more.

The Ford Model T assembly line, where bodies are being mated to chassis. *Detroit Public Library Lincoln Highway Digital Archive*

Model T construction progressed from the Piquette Avenue plant, where cars were essentially hand produced, to the Highland Park plant, where the first modern assembly line was put into use. Components traveled throughout the plant while stationary workers installed them over and over and over. Such workers were a key part of the manufacturing process, but certainly the boredom factor must have been intense. However, the company was producing more cars than any other manufacturer on earth, and the fact that employees earned a $5 salary per eight-hour day not only made the boredom tolerable but meant they could purchase a Model T Ford themselves—unheard of at the time. To develop his assembly line, Ford used meat-packing plants for his blueprint, though he had to reconfigure the process in reverse since the meat plants were, in effect, disassembly plants. Even though Highland Park was viewed by outsiders as a manufacturing marvel, it was seen as obsolete and cramped by those working on the inside.

In order to keep producing cars at such a massive scale, Ford envisioned an even larger industrial complex, one where raw materials came in one end and finished cars drove out the other. Construction of the massive Rouge assembly plant began in 1917 and was completed near the end of Model T production. It was admired by capitalists, scholars, and political figures around the world, including such controversial figures as Josef Stalin and Adolf Hitler.

From virtually the beginning of the Model T era, Henry Ford argued with his critics, and with his son, Edsel, that the car was not outdated, and that it should not be replaced. But sales were rapidly declining as the buying public desired more style and comfort in their automobiles. Sales of competitive vehicles increased at Ford's expense.

The last Model T rolled off the assembly line in 1927, and after five months of assembly-line upgrades and retooling, the first Model As began to emerge from the Rouge plant.

The reign of the century's most significant automobile had finally come to an end.

Gulf or Sunoco 260—was flowing, that attendant washed your windshield. And if you asked, he might check your tire pressure as well. Oh, and fuel was less than $1 per gallon, sometimes only 25 or 50 cents.

Fast-forward to the same experience today. Depending on the season and how much OPEC is regulating prices, the gas can be as much as $4 per gallon. Want your windshield washed? Do it yourself, buddy—*if* the squeegee and cleaning fluid are in the trough. And you can top off your own tires, thank you, but only if you insert 25 or 50 cents or $1 into a little machine on the far side of the property. Then a lot of noise produces a Mickey Mouse current of air.

The proud employees? They're inside the Mini Mart, sometimes behind bulletproof glass, dispensing cigarettes and Coke Zero and gas-station hot dogs, and working for a minimum-wage salary.

Unfortunately, the pride is gone from every end of the gas-buying experience except for the CEO and those shareholders, who, after stripping away every dignity for consumers and low-level employees, are making more money than ever.

Early travelers had to make their own lodging provisions when driving cross-country on the Lincoln Highway. Some slept in their cars, some in tents, and some, like this couple, threw a tarp across their car and slept next to it. *Lincoln Highway Digital Image Collection, University of Michigan Library (Special Collections Library)*

28. Before embarking on this trip, there were two states in the United States I had never visited: North Dakota and Nebraska. Now there is just one.

When we entered Nebraska, we headed directly to Lincoln. In addition to being the state capital, Lincoln was also the city where that evening we were to be "honored," for lack of a better word.

How best to say this . . . I'd rather be lucky than good? Timing is everything?

THE MODEL T'S IMPACT ON SOCIETY

"I will build a motor car for the great multitude," Henry Ford was quoted as saying in an article that was featured in the tenth anniversary issue of *Ford Times* magazine in June 1913. "It will be large enough for the family, but small enough for the individual to run and care for. It will be constructed of the best materials, by the best men to be hired, after the simplest designs that modern engineering can devise. It will be so low in price that no man making a good salary will be unable to own one, and enjoy with his family the blessing of hours of pleasure in God's greatest open spaces."

It is believed that Ford first used the quotation in 1903, at the founding of Ford Motor Company. How insightful.

The genius of Ford Motor Company provided an affordable set of wheels for the world, but the Model T actually changed the world in the process. Until its release, workers, farmers, and those bypassed by the automotive age were denied motorized transport because of the high cost of entry. Humorist Will Rogers said that Henry Ford had changed the habits of more people than Caesar, Mussolini, Charlie Chaplin, Clara Bow, Xerxes, Amos and Andy, and Bernard Shaw.

For the first time, automobile ownership became a reality for the average worker. The vehicle's cost dropped from $850, its price when it was introduced in 1908, to less than $300 in 1925. Model T ownership provided the freedom to travel further than most consumers imagined before, and for a minimal investment. Owners regularly boasted that operating expenses were less than $100 a year.

The Model T was simple and reliable, and driving one was easily mastered. With its ease of operation and low purchase price, it was truly the car that brought Americans, and indeed the world, out of the horse-and-buggy age and into the horseless-carriage era that we still, at least for now, enjoy today.

The car made traveling vacations possible, with many owners adapting various camping methods involving the car. Some called the T a Ford Hotel and even used the folding upper portion of the windshield as a dining table. Certainly the so-called Vagabonds helped promote that image, as the foursome—Henry Ford, Thomas Edison, Harvey Firestone, and John Burroughs—regularly used Model Ts to camp around the United States.

The cars became tireless workhorses on farms, not only because they gave rural farmers a means to more easily travel to markets, but also because the cars could be adapted to plow fields, power sawmills, and move grain into elevators.

Women, who had the reputation of often finding motor-vehicle operation too complicated, quickly adapted to the easy controls of a Model T. Suddenly women had the ability to travel for pleasure or to work outside of their homes. One woman bragged that her Model T allowed her to work in the farm fields in the morning, bring her home to perform her housework in the afternoon, and then take her 35 miles to see a band concert in the city that evening.

As author David Brinkley wrote in his brilliant book *Wheels for the World* in 2003, "With the possible exception of the Singer sewing machine, no US-made mechanical device had ever been so widely distributed around the world." *Ford Times* in 1910 said the cars were sold in Kuala Lumpur, Turkey, and far-flung islands such as Barbados, Mauritius, and Newfoundland.

Whether Henry Ford fully foresaw the Model T's success was when he conceived it in 1908, or whether it was simply luck and timing, he remains a folk hero more than a century later.

SPEEDWAY MOTORS' MUSEUM OF AMERICAN SPEED

The Museum of American Speed in Lincoln, Nebraska, was opened in 1992 by "Speedy" Bill and Joyce Smith. It provided Speedy, a lifelong auto-racing enthusiast and founder of the Speedway Motors high-performance parts business, with a way to share his passion with other enthusiasts.

Smith's lifelong collection of hot rods and Indy, NASCAR, midget, and drag-racing cars from the 1920s until the present is displayed in a modern, three-level, 150,000-square-foot building.

They are an amazing sight, but I was not prepared for the engine and accessories exhibit. Hundreds, maybe thousands, of rare racing engines and one-of-a-kind accessories—many I had never seen before—are displayed in period and thematic settings. I could have spent hours more just looking at the engines and reading the display cards.

Imagine double-overhead-cam racing cylinder heads developed more than one hundred years ago for the humble Model T Ford! These bits looked positively exotic and seemed like they would have been at home on an Alfa Romeo or a Ferrari, yet they were developed for cars like our *Something*. Just amazing.

Smith also assembled collections of toy cars and pedal cars, karts, memorabilia, photos, and automobilia.

In addition to the displays, the museum hosts an annual festival for vintage race cars. Limited to vehicles with four-cylinder engines built before 1935, it includes a 150-mile tour on rural country roads, a competitive hillclimb, and an opportunity for owners to tune their machines on the museum's chassis dynamometer. Called the International Speedsters Trial and Reunion, the June event attracts enthusiasts from around the United States and around the world.

The Museum of American Speed should be on every car enthusiast's bucket list. Check out www.museumofamericanspeed.com.

While planning the trip, I had been communicating with Mike Vaughn, president of the Model T Ford Club of America and a resident of Lincoln. Mike had been kind enough to give me names, phone numbers, and e-mail addresses of Model T Club members who lived along or near the Lincoln Highway throughout the United States, just in case we had an issue.

"If you need a place to work on your car, or parts, we have a bunch of guys who would love to help you out," he told me. Thankfully, up to that point, we hadn't had to use any of those contacts yet.

But Mike and I decided we needed to meet each other as we passed through Nebraska. The city of Lincoln is not on the Lincoln Highway, funnily enough, so we would dip south from Highway 30 once we hit Fremont and head south on Highway 77. I had called Mike a couple of days before to give him a report on our progress and inform him we were one day ahead of schedule and should be in Lincoln on Saturday night.

"I don't believe your timing," he said. "The Nebraskaland Model T Club is celebrating its fiftieth anniversary on Saturday night at the Museum of American Speed. Do you think you can make it?"

Of course we could!

So we had *Something* barreling down the road, at one point hitting 59 miles per hour, a new record speed for us. Mike encouraged us to arrive at 5:00 p.m. and said that we could drive the car right into the museum's dining room and participate in the dinner.

Our timing couldn't have been better; because of traffic and distance, we arrived about ten minutes later than we planned—fashionably late. Just as all the attendees might have thought we were blowing them off, we came around the corner with our *ahooooga* horn blasting.

We pulled through the museum's garage door and right into the middle of the dinner!

Mike had arranged seating for the three of us at the head table. We had a nice dinner, and then I was asked to give a little talk about our trip so far. I told the audience that our amazing car had not missed a beat, that we had met amazing people because we drove such an interesting vehicle, and that we had seen amazing sights thus far along the Lincoln Highway.

Then, of course, the club had its own business to take care of: fifty years of Model T memories, photos, and funny stories. It was a nice dinner, but for us, our evening was far from over.

As I noted earlier in this book, I am on the advisory board for McPherson College's automotive restoration program.

Every old-car enthusiast should breathe a sigh of relief that the students in this program are the future of our hobby. Graduates are often recruited to intern and work at some of the top restoration shops, museums, and private collections around the United States. Some have even opened their own restoration businesses.

The school is located in McPherson, Kansas—which, as it happens, is about four hours south of Lincoln. Program administrator Brian Martin, himself a Model T enthusiast who drives his touring car to the school daily regardless of weather or temperature, had offered to bring five students to perform a

We drove *Something* right into the banquet room of the Museum of American Speed in Lincoln, Nebraska. The Nebraskaland Model T Club was having their fiftieth anniversary dinner celebration and invited us to join their festivities.

After dinner, *Something* was brought into the museum's workshop where five students and their professor from McPherson College's automotive restoration program were set loose on the car, performing a pit stop at our trip's halfway point.

"pit stop" on *Something* in the museum workshop while we were there. So after dinner, while Brian observed from a distance, Dave managed the group of students as they changed the oil in the engine and transmission, changed a headlight sealed beam that had burned out, adjusted the low and reverse transmission bands, checked the rear brake hydraulics, and lubricated critical locations in the suspension, driveline, and valvetrain. He then gave a practical lesson on metallurgy, machining, and the intricacies of the Model T. He told the students that a Model T front axle can be twisted six times without breaking—and to prove it, showed them a T axle the museum had on display that had, in fact, been twisted six times.

"Henry Ford used the best metals available," he said.

While students Austin Hiebert, Phillip Reinhardt, Jared Thurston, Mike Cowan, and Gary Irwin worked on *Something*, Brian and I made a run to buy oil and other parts. After performing the pit stop, which took a couple of hours, the students were invited to tour the museum with museum docent Rich Johnston.

The place is amazing. Cofounder Bill "Speedy" Smith spent a lifetime accumulating custom engines and accessories for Model Ts and As, flathead Fords, Hemis, and Chevys. It was a nice end to a long day.

We arrived at our hotel late, but I felt worse for Brian Martin and his van load of students, who had to drive four hours back to McPherson. Those students had to take their semester final exams on Monday, so they needed all day Sunday to study.

We arrived at the Cornhusker Hotel in downtown Lincoln, which had been recommended to us by Model T Club President Mike Vaughn, at about 11:00 p.m. On the way there, we almost ran out of gas again; we were on fumes and took 10.68 gallons into our 10-gallon tank when we refueled. Obviously the Nebraska winds had affected our mileage.

It hadn't been our longest driving day, but it was certainly our most physically challenging.

29. It rained overnight, and the streets were still wet when I hit the pavement the next morning. We had decided to take a day off from the road to regroup, sleep late, do our laundry, organize the cars, and tour the city of Lincoln.

This is the fifth book that Michael and I have collaborated on, and on every trip we take, we get totally burned out working from dawn to after dark traveling, interviewing, and photographing. Every time we finish one, we promise the next one will be different. We say, "Next time we'll take a day off in the middle of the trip." But we never do.

This time we did, and it felt so good!

The next day we'd hit the road with new energy, refreshed and ready to complete the second half of our journey. But today . . . ahh.

It was Mother's Day, so I called my wife, Pat, and my mom to send them love on their special day. Then I took off for a run through Lincoln. I was training for the New York Marathon at the time, so I tried to practice a few miles every couple of days while on this trip. My run that day took me through Lincoln's commercial, residential, industrial, and historic districts.

Fuel:
96.1 GALLONS
Distance:
1,733 MILES

It's amazing how an early Sunday-morning run so often gives me a good idea of the character of a place. I've run through cities and towns around the United States, South America, and Europe, and it's my little tourism secret.

One Sunday morning in 2012, I ran from the northern edge of Manhattan, where it meets the Bronx, 13 miles down Fifth Avenue to Wall Street. It was an amazing experience to see the city wake up at 5:00 a.m. Weekend workers in upper Manhattan were out buying their coffee, donuts, and newspapers; churchgoers in their Sunday best were walking to services where choirs were already singing; café owners were hosing off the sidewalks and preparing to serve brunch; and retail businesses toward Midtown were putting out their wares. The financial district, meanwhile, was absolutely closed until Monday morning.

A personal tour like that shows the good, the bad, and the ugly. The elegance and the grittiness is out there for all to see, without pedestrians or traffic to block the view.

Lincoln, Nebraska, was not as dramatic as Manhattan, I should note. It's a nice town with clean streets and folks sitting on their front porches drinking their early-morning coffee.

"Good morning," some said as I plodded past.

I particularly enjoyed running through the historic Haymarket District, a funky, repurposed part of the city near the Pinnacle Bank Arena that is transitioning from industrial to urban cool. Neat coffee shops, pubs, and restaurants occupy spaces that were once brick warehouses and manufacturing plants. It reminded me of the Pearl District in Portland, Oregon, where industry and hip lifestyle businesses coexist side by side. I hadn't realized that Lincoln was so funky and diverse.

Many times while on my morning jogs I also look for old cars in people's yards and driveways, but I found none that morning.

By the time I got back to the Cornhusker Hotel, I had clocked 6 miles at a 9:54 pace, not a speed I would have been proud of a few years ago, but at sixty-four years old, I'm just glad to still be running.

30. Dave told Michael and me he had a treat for us that afternoon—to host us at one of his favorite museums on the planet, the Strategic

STRATEGIC AIR COMMAND AND AEROSPACE MUSEUM

This museum is located along I-80 in Ashland, Nebraska, just east of Lincoln. It was originally located in eastern Nebraska, on the former Offutt Air Force Base, which became headquarters for the Strategic Air Command (SAC) in 1948. SAC head general Curtis LeMay's vision in 1959 of a museum that preserved historic aircraft was realized when the first plane was put on display.

Initially airplanes were displayed outdoors, but to keep them from being damaged by the elements, the museum was moved to its more accessible present location. Walking into the expansive atrium, visitors immediately encounter the massive Lockheed SR-71 Blackbird, which hangs from the ceiling. Beyond the lobby, the 300,000-square-foot building goes off in two directions designed to resemble two adjoining aircraft hangers. Additionally, there is a children's area, a snack bar, and a two hundred seat theater.

Presently thirty-one planes of various vintage are on permanent display, with planes from other museums occasionally swapped for special displays. Some of those on display include the Boeing B-17G Flying Fortress, B-29 Superfortress, McDonnell RF-4C Phantom, and Lockheed U-2C Dragon Lady. Additionally, rockets and missiles are on view outside the building.

The exhibits are immense and intriguing. Even if you, like me, are not a serious aircraft enthusiast, this place is a must see if traveling on I-80 through Nebraska.

Air Command (SAC) and Aerospace Museum in Ashland, Nebraska, just northeast of Lincoln. We were all in.

We had a leisurely morning and lunch at a microbrewery in the Haymarket district, then Dave drove us in the Escape to the SAC Museum, off I-80. We decided to leave *Something* in the hotel garage, allowing it a day of vacation as well.

The value of visiting this museum became apparent the moment we drove through the front gate: a huge, camouflaged F-105 Thunderchief jet bomber greets visitors as they walk up the driveway. Entering the building, the feeling of awe is further reinforced.

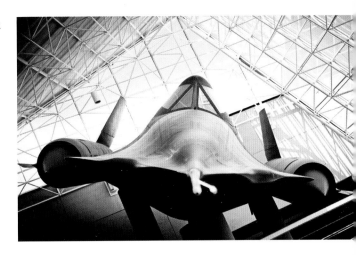

We were greeted by this massive sight when Dave brought us to one of his favorite museums, the Strategic Air Command Museum in Ashland, Nebraska. This Lockheed 771 Blackbird, now retired, is the fastest military plane ever built, having flown across the United States in just over one hour.

Seemingly floating in space above us in the lobby was the sexiest, stealthiest jet in the world staring us right in the face. It's a Lockheed SR-71 Blackbird, and it's a beautiful piece of sculpture to behold. This spy plane never carried a single bomb or even a machine gun; it was developed purely for the purpose of photographing the earth from very high altitudes. And to go very fast. We learned that the Blackbird flew at the edge of space at speeds near Mach 3, about 2,200 miles per hour.

The Blackbird was retired in 1999, with one West Coast–based example designated for installation in the Smithsonian Museum in Washington, D.C. As it was being prepared for the flight from L.A. to D.C., the pilots were challenged to set a cross-country speed record.

Guess how long it took? Less time than it takes many people to commute to work: sixty-seven minutes.

Amazing. At an average speed of just over 1,800 miles per hour, it is estimated the Blackbird could circle the globe in less than two hours.

The rest of the museum is packed with amazing military prop and jet aircraft as well as helicopters. If you're passing through Lincoln, it's worth spending a few hours there. Thanks for the treat, Dave.

31. The next morning was beautiful. The forecast, which had initially threatened thunder showers, had been updated to partly cloudy and 90 degrees.

It had been ten days since I last shaved, deciding that the weight and bulk of a razor was too much to take on an adventure like this. Besides, looking like a gruff traveler was more in keeping with driving a Model T across the country. The same theory probably wouldn't work if we were driving a new Lexus.

My neck was starting to get itchy, though. Guys like my son, Brian, and race driver Tony Stewart, who regularly go ten days at a time, look like studs when they do. Sadly, the same theory doesn't work for this old man. I wondered what Pat was going to say when Gentle Ben came walking through the door in a couple of weeks.

We had been spoiled in South Bend with our police escort out of town. Leaving Lincoln during Monday-morning rush hour, we had to find our own way out of city, and had to actually stop at red lights—the indignity! Our GPS tried to force us to take I-80, but we were determined to take Highway 34 west so we could get back onto Highway 30, the Lincoln Highway. This only reinforced my concern for future travelers, the idea that regardless of where we want to go and how we want to get there, GPS or the driverless car could force us to take the route it wants us to go. And those travelers will sit powerlessly in the passenger compartment, for who are they to argue? I mean, as long as they can watch the latest *Fast and the Furious* movie while commuting around the landscape, who cares what they're passing?

Regardless, our rejuvenation day in Lincoln was much needed. It allowed us to recharge our internal batteries, and we were ready to get back on the road.

. . . .

32. Obviously, we did not invent the cross-country drive in a primitive car; we simply added our names to a long list of previous efforts. The first ocean-to-ocean assault was undertaken in 1903 by Vermont doctor Horatio Jackson.

Jackson made a $50 bet that he could drive from San Francisco to New York in an automobile. Alcohol may have been involved, especially considering Jackson didn't even own a car at the time. Nonetheless, he immediately purchased a used two-seater Winton 20-horsepower automobile, and three days later, he took off for the East Coast—along with hired mechanic Sewell Crocker and a goggle-wearing dog called Bud—by heading north. They wisely decided that going through Oregon and Idaho would be less difficult than tackling the Sierra Nevadas and the Rocky Mountains.

Sixty-five days later (forty-five days of driving, twenty days of car repairs and waiting for parts), the threesome arrived in New York, having driven almost 6,000 miles. One only hopes that Jackson collected on his $50 wager.

Jackson's driving adventures are well chronicled in a Ken Burns's documentary film *Horatio's Drive* and in a book of the same name, coauthored by Burns and Dayton Duncan.

After Jackson proved the country could be crossed by automobile, many adventurous motorists began making the trip, either east to west or west to east. Some saw it as the adventure of a lifetime, similar to hiking the Appalachian Trail today. Some were moving from one coast to the other and undertook the journey for practical reasons. And still others represented car companies sponsoring the trip as a marketing exercise, seeing it as a unique way to showcase the reliability of their products to consumers. In fact, just a month after the Jackson party departed San Francisco, a Packard-sponsored team also left San Francisco for New York, deciding on a more direct, albeit more difficult route. The Packard team arrived in New York sixty-two days later, three days faster than Jackson's time.

Henry Ford's son, Edsel, made a road trip from Detroit to San Francisco as a twenty-one-year-old in 1915. Six equally privileged friends joined him in what was seen by their parents as a rite of passage before the responsibilities of adulthood took hold. Of course, he drove one of his family's products, a Model T, but his friends drove a Cadillac and a Stutz. The 2,400-mile trip took five weeks; there is no evidence that anyone on the road trip was in a particular hurry to reach California.

Edsel kept meticulous notes and took many photographs along their journey. One hundred years later, two historians—Historic Vehicle Association (HVA) president Mark Gessler and HVA historian Casey Maxon—recreated Edsel's trip in a 1915 Model T Touring Car, virtually identical to Edsel's. The team pored over Edsel's notes and studied his photos in an attempt to exactly replicate the route he and his friends had taken a century earlier. Since roads were not as plentiful in 1915 as they are now, the younger Ford and his friends

We never did touch base with Utica Bill, who has a nice collection of vintage tin just west of Lincoln. The sign on his door simply said "sick today," so we were left to imagine what cars were out of our sight (and how much he might be selling them for . . .).

There are plenty more where they came from. Gibbons Fiberglass founder Dwight Bond lined up a few of his extra Ford pickups for an auction he was holding. Dwight started making fiberglass bodies for hot rods decades ago, eventually selling the business to his son, Kyle.

asked permission from farmers to drive across their fields and pastures. In 2015, Gessler and Maxon attempted the same "close the gate behind you" agenda.

Seeing photos from Edsel's 1915 trip, we noticed the camping youths were all dressed in suits with vests and ties. Dave and I were pretty underdressed by comparison in our shorts and T-shirts.

33. Driving down the Lincoln Highway without stopping every few miles required some restraint on my part.

If you've read any of my other books, you know that finding old cars is my life's calling. These old vehicles are called barn finds: cars, trucks, and motorcycles that have been neglected and ignored for a number of years. There is nothing I enjoy doing more than discovering cars that are often hidden in plain sight. Since the point of this trip was not barn finding, however, I exhibited an amazing amount of self-control on the occasions I spotted interesting cars hiding behind fences and inside barns we passed.

But passing Utica Bill's was more than I could handle. I had to stop.

On Highway 34, just west of Lincoln, was a fenced-in yard that ranks right up there with some of my best discoveries. It was connected to a body shop called Utica Bill's. I walked up to the office to discuss the old cars, but a note on the door said simply "sick today." Utica Bill was obviously under the weather, so I called both the office phone and the cell phone listed on the sign and left a message. Usually in this instance, I would respectfully start inspecting the cars, keeping my hands in my pockets at all times and my car parked prominently out front in order to give the impression that I am not hiding anything. But the fences around Utica Bill's yard were too high and foreboding, so I decided just to peek over the top.

From what I could see, there were quite a number of cool projects. I'm guessing there were about a hundred cars in the lot. Here is a partial list of what I could see over the fence:

Henry Js (three)
Late-1940s Buicks and Pontiacs (lots, leading me to believe there was a major GM dealer in town)
Ramblers (several)
Dodge Suburban two-door wagon
Ford Rancheros, a 1957 and a Falcon
Studebakers (several)
Ford Starliners (1960 and 1961)
Corvairs (several)
1931 Chevy
1952 Ford Ranch Wagon (similar to the '53 I have at home)
1966 Mercury Comet drag car
1963 Ford Fairlane Hardtop

And lots more I couldn't see well enough to identify. I was hoping Bill would call me back, but unfortunately he never did.

34. The constant Nebraska winds continued to reinforce the fact that Sandy from Colo hadn't been kidding. I don't know if this continues year-round, but I can see issues with planting seeds and plowing snow that would be made more difficult with the constant blowing. The flags we passed were standing straight out. It may have been the result of the threatened thunderstorms in the forecast.

Other powerful winds we experienced were manmade.

Those came from the huge eastbound semitrucks traveling on Highway 34 at high speeds, which nearly knocked *Something* into the ditch. The winds buffeting off those trucks, especially when they were traveling in tandem, required several degrees of steering correction to keep our 1,800-pound car on the road. Driving a fragile T in one direction while high-speed trucks traveled in the opposite, was one hazard I'm sure early Model T travelers did not have to deal with.

Fuel:
103 GALLONS
Distance:
1,898 MILES

We stopped to fill up *Something* at a Sinclair gas station in Grand Island that included everything we have come to expect these days at filling stations: fuel, restrooms, a convenience store, and a snack bar . . . oh, and Dr. John's Lingerie and Adult Novelty Boutique.

I'm trying to think of something clever to say here without being offensive or sexist, but words escape me. So we'll just leave it at that.

· ·

35. It's a good thing I don't own a Model T of my own, because I might have considered making this journey by myself. That would have been a big mistake.

I clearly don't have the practical mechanical knowledge and ability to keep a car like this on the road. That's why Dave was such a savior. At every fuel stop or lunch break, he was under the car and under the hood with a wrench in his hand. Dave knows cars well, and this one in particular—down to the last nut and bolt.

It's amazing how little I knew about my codriver before committing to drive across the country with him. As we traversed the prairielands of Nebraska, I asked him about his life.

Dave Coleman was born in Catonsville, a suburb of Baltimore, Maryland. He is the only child of Margret, whose parents emigrated from Germany, and Richard, a World War II veteran of English descent.

Dave obviously was bitten by the car bug early, because as a young kid he would regularly accompany his father to the Sinclair gas station he owned.

"I got my hands dirty at a very young age helping my dad around the shop," said Dave. "At ten years old, I saw the movie *Thunder Road* with Robert Mitchum and instantly fell in love with Shoebox Fords [1949–1951], which were the stars of the movie."

Soon he found a 1949 Ford with the engine sitting in the trunk, which he bought for $10. He installed a larger Mercury engine and sold it for $100. The hook was set, and Dave was officially in the car business.

When he got his driver's license at eighteen, he bought a 1959 English Ford called an Anglia, which was powered by a four-cylinder flathead engine. With the help of his dad, he converted the Anglia into a hot rod by installing a four-cylinder Chevy Nova engine.

After high school, a six-year stint in the army made Dave into an accomplished machinist. He opened a machine shop, Performance Engineering, in 1972 and has been in business ever since.

"In 1976 I bought a Porsche Carrera speedster race car from driver Bruce Jennings for $16,000," he said. "It was an absurd amount of money at the time."

Decades later, he sold that Porsche for many times the purchase price, proving the old vintage car adage that you can never pay too much—you can only buy too soon. It turned out to be a good investment after all, although he didn't buy it for that reason.

Dave eventually moved from Baltimore to Summit Point, West Virginia, to get away from what he calls "the crush. "

"I grew up with the 695 Baltimore Beltway just one house away from my house," he said. "The noise became too much to handle. [In West Virginia] the pace of life is much slower, and I'm surrounded by history.

"When I came to West Virginia, it was like a time warp. I bought 22 acres of forest and set up my home and business there. It used to be in Baltimore, people would give me the finger. Now, people wave at me."

Of course, living near a racetrack is a plus. He has won numerous racing championships, including four in a row with his 2-liter Porsche 911.

Today Dave provides complete service to all sorts of cars, but he specializes in Porsches. He enjoys engine building but also sets up suspensions and installs roll cages. He has a large collection of cars and parts—again, mostly Porsches, but also a couple of Studebakers, Ford hot rods, and another Model T speedster that's more radical than *Something*.

"Of course, Model Ts were the most important cars of all time," says Dave. "They changed everything."

Kyle and his dog in one of his new fiberglass hot rods, a chopped 1933/34 Ford Tudor sedan. Besides producing fiberglass, Kyle enjoys building hot rods from the ground up. He said most of his business comes from the Lincoln, Nebraska, area.

36. We were driving along the railroad tracks, as we had done on much of the Lincoln Highway, when we entered the town of Gibbon, Nebraska. On the right side was one of those barn-find scenes that had me call out to Dave, "Stop!"

We pulled over to take a closer look at some of those rusty relics I love so much. Behind and next to an old gas station were forty-nine—I counted them, *forty-nine*—old Ford pickup trucks and cabs. A couple of trucks were complete, but most were simply cabs either on a chassis or by themselves. A sign was posted next to the building:

PUBLIC AUCTION

SATURDAY, MAY 27

CLASSIC CARS AND PARTS

ENGINES, TRANS, TOOLS AND EQUIP.

Intriguing, but nobody was around. So as Michael was shooting photos, I went to explore some more old cars on the other side of the railroad tracks. It seemed to be another old-car shop, but this one was open and employees were inside working away on a variety of relics.

I met Kyle Bond, who owns the company that his father founded decades earlier, Gibbon Fiberglass Bodies.

I'm a hot rodder, and I've never owned a Gibbon '32 Ford body, but I certainly know of them. This little town in rural Nebraska has made national and probably international impact in the hot-rod industry since Kyle's father, Dwight, started the business in 1971. Gibbon Fiberglass Bodies from Gibbon, Nebraska; now it all made sense.

"My father did restorations and started making Model A Ford fenders because the ones he found were too rough," said Kyle, who bought the business from his dad in 1996. After Model A fenders, Dwight started reproducing '32, '33, and '34 Ford bodies. Now Kyle still produces these bodies, but his passion lies more in building complete cars. While Dwight was totally into bodies, his son enjoys the upholstery, painting, and mechanical aspects of hot rods.

"My father has always been into F-100 Fords, so those are all his across the tracks," said Kyle. "He's going to sell a bunch of them soon at an auction."

Dwight himself is pretty much retired from the day-to-day hot rod business, but he has a hobby shop across the tracks in a new metal building where he keeps his private stash of hot rods and projects. We had lunch in Gibbon at a little restaurant owned by a guy with a voice just like the late racing broadcaster Chris Economaki.

"Try the meatloaf on the buffet," he said. "It's from my mother's recipe. I've been serving it for thirty years."

Having made a couple of new hot-rod friends and enjoyed a delicious $5 meatloaf lunch, we pulled out of town. A roadside sign read, "Thanks for visiting Gibbon, Your Smile City."

Me when I'm hungry! Just a few blocks from the Bond's Gibbon Fiberglass plant was a little restaurant that offered a Mom's Meatloaf Recipe buffet lunch for only $5. It was terrific.

37. At 88 degrees, this was our hottest day yet, though we lucked out, seeing as the forecast was for 92 degrees. The clouds overhead kept the heat at bay.

It was quite a change from the 33 degrees we'd experienced in Pennsylvania, a 55-degree variance. We could easily exceed those temps, both lower and higher, once we pushed into Wyoming and Nevada.

But for the time being we were sitting pretty with our 1926 air conditioning: Dave pushed the bottom of the windshield out to give us nice blow-through ventilation action at 54 miles per hour.

BURMA-SHAVE BILLBOARDS

I've never met anybody who didn't enjoy the clever billboards that were installed by the Burma-Shave company from the 1920s until the 1960s. Burma-Shave, a brushless brand of shaving cream, was developed by the Burma-Vita Company of Minneapolis. Sales were weak, so the company sought a way to increase its exposure.

The company rolled out a highway billboard campaign in its home state in 1926, which was expanded into nearly all of the contiguous states except New Mexico, Nevada, and Arizona (too little population), and Massachusetts (too expensive to advertise).

The campaign was always the same: six boards spaced appropriately apart so that motorists could read the message on the first five boards at rural highway speeds. The last board always showed the Burma-Shave logo. The billboards were written to deliver their message on one of two themes—good grooming or highway safety—usually in twenty words or less. Sales grew, making Burma-Shave the second-best-selling brushless shaving cream in the country.

When the Interstate Highway System was established in 1956, the higher speeds made the billboards harder to safely read and comprehend. When the Burma-Shave brand was sold to Phillip Morris in 1963, the once-successful billboard campaign ended.

Today, examples of the classic advertising boards are displayed in a number of museums around the country—the Henry Ford in Dearborn, Michigan, for example—as well as in rural towns and private lands in an attempt to entertain motorists with the nostalgic program. We passed a number of them along the Lincoln Highway over the course of our trip, and they were a pleasure to read and kept boredom at bay.

In all, six hundred Burma-Shave boards were written and displayed during the program's four-decade run. Here are a few of my favorites:

A guy/Who drives/A car wide open
Is not thinkin'/He's just hopin'

His cheek/Was rough/His chick vamoosed
And now she won't/Come home to roost

Doesn't kiss you/Like she useter?
Perhaps she's seen/A smoother rooster!!

He tried/To cross/As fast train neared
Death didn't draft him/He volunteered

Altho insured/Remember, kiddo
They don't pay you/They pay your widow

Why is it/When you try to pass
The guy in front/Goes twice as fast?

Dinah doesn't/Treat him right
But if he'd shave/Dyna-mite!

The safest rule/No ifs or buts
Just drive/Like every one else/Is nuts!

38. For generations, the unofficial halfway point on the Lincoln Highway was the 1733 Ranch, just west of Kearney, Nebraska. The logic was this: from the ranch, it was 1,733 miles to San Francisco and 1,733 to Boston.

There is a major flaw with this formula, though. The Lincoln Highway begins in New York City, not Boston. Basically, this farmer had a ranch that he wanted to make into a tourist destination, but it wasn't exactly in the middle of the Lincoln Highway. He could either move his ranch 30 miles to the west or he could "alter" the Lincoln Highway's starting point to make his calculations work. He chose the latter, and to this day folks believe the 1733 Ranch is a motorist landmark.

Except it's not.

Now, I may not be the sharpest knife in the drawer, but I knew we didn't begin this adventure in Boston. With a little help from Brian Butko, author of the terrific book *Greetings from the Lincoln Highway* (which I used as a travel guide every day along this journey) and Paul Gilger, a historian who maps and leads Lincoln Highway tour groups, we set the record straight. The actual Lincoln Highway midway point is west of Kearney in the town of Cozad. Paul sent a satellite photo so we could zero in at the exact location.

Fuel:
111.87 GALLONS
Distance:
2,061 MILES

"The midpoint of the Lincoln Highway is on the corner of East Eighth Street and Main Street, across from the entrance of the Hi-Gain Feed lot," Paul texted me.

Perfect.

We located a change in pavement across from the Hi-Gain entrance, where the surface went from asphalt to a paved stone surface. So we designated that pavement change as the official spot where we were 1,694.5 miles to New York City and 1,694.5 to the Golden Gate Bridge.

One side of the pavement line was, in theory, the East Coast, and the other side was the West Coast. We were as far from the Atlantic Ocean as we were from the Pacific Ocean. More importantly, we were halfway to our destination!

This was a significant moment for your happy Model T threesome—OK, foursome if we count *Something*, who I don't want to leave out. When we reached this point, we had actually driven 2,012 miles, about 300 more than the official highway mileage. This can be explained by our detours "off-track" (remember, we were never actually lost) in the confusing areas of southern New Jersey and Philadelphia where signage was either confusing or nonexistent.

As Michael was taking photographs at this landmark, the farmer who owned the adjacent field came driving up on his huge John Deere tractor. He wondered what all the hoopla was about; a Model T Ford and a photographer in the road in front of his property was probably more excitement than usually goes on there. We explained how his property was a quasi-landmark.

"You should install a sign, and maybe open a T-shirt and souvenir shop to celebrate your good fortune," I told him. He said he would consider it, but not for at least a year or two.

39.

Something had not missed a beat on the trip's first half. It ran strong, handled well, and, in Model T terms, has lots of power.

The car has been lowered on its suspension, giving it sporty handling more similar to the English-built MG TD that I have at home in my garage than a century-old automobile. My MG was built in 1952, twenty-six years after this T rolled off Henry Ford's assembly line in Detroit, Michigan. On twisty roads, by comparison, this must be the best-handling Model T in the world.

It's pretty comfortable to sit in, too, thanks to the modified interior that owner Nathan had installed just for this trip. But once we were in the cockpit, sitting almost in the fetal position, we didn't want to leave too often.

Getting out after two or three hours, by which point our bodies had taken a "set," was a bit of a chore. Once our muscles became comfortable with this condensed seating position, they were reluctant to move without a fair amount of coaxing.

Verbal "ooohs" and "ouches" could be heard every time Dave and I extricated ourselves from the cockpit. And a bit of stretching ensued before we could walk to the gas pump or hotel lobby.

Something had been an amazing partner on our trip so far—like an old, reliable pet who marks its territory with oil and water. And like a happy old golden retriever, it wagged a tail in the form of the flagpole we'd installed as a safety precaution as we motored down the road.

One of those Lincoln Highway landmarks that is still standing after half a century. Companies just don't use billboards like this anymore, so it's important that we honor the grand old signs that still remain.

Mountain Standard Time 3

Parked at the Bonneville Salt Flats in Utah, we've traveled a long way from our starting point in Times Square but have not left the Lincoln Highway.

....

1. We stopped for the night in the town of Ogallala, Nebraska. It was 8:00 p.m., a good time to call it quits for the day.

While checking in at our modern, generic chain hotel, I saw a sign in the lobby that said, "You Are Now in the Mountain Time Zone." Our third time zone! Suddenly it was only 7:00. Love those free hours!

Dave decided to go shopping at the Walmart across the highway and grab dinner on his own, so Michael and I were on our own to search for the town's best meal. Near the interstate there were the standard chain restaurants, but we wanted to experience something more local.

En route, we noticed some ominous clouds to the west. I wondered aloud whether a storm was coming in our direction.

We decided on a saloon-looking place called the Front Street Steakhouse and Crystal Palace Saloon. A saloon sounded just right for a couple of hard-riding cowpokes like us—but if we had hopes of fist fights and gun battles breaking out at the bar, we were about to be disappointed. When we walked into the bar, we found at least twenty high-school and college students in full rehearsal mode for their summer performing jobs.

During the summer season, diners are treated to wholesome off-Broadway productions at the Crystal Palace, and students must qualify to secure a performing position. Once selected, there are many rehearsals before the show begins in June, which at the time of our visit was still a month away.

These students were serious and professional. They were singing and dancing a tune about the town of Ogallala and living in the Wild West. It was terrific dinner theater for Michael and me as we watched these young people practice their parts over and over. Watching a Broadway-type production in the making was not what we planned on experiencing—steak and beer would have been fine—but it was the perfect opportunity to experience this local culture.

"The Crystal Palace Review is the longest-running summer stock theater in Nebraska," said Kathleen Bauer, who owns the establishment along with her husband. "It's been running every year since 1964, a year after the bar, restaurant, museum, and cabaret opened."

Soon after we got back to the hotel from dinner, the sky opened up. Remember that storm we saw brewing en route to dinner? Pouring rain, hail, lightning, and thunder made for quite a sky show. Luckily, Dave had returned from shopping, and *Something* was safely parked under the hotel's front entry.

2. Luckily for our drive, the night's torrential rains gave way to a beautifully sunny and mild morning. But while eating breakfast, we noticed on the television that there could be additional weather events to the west that we might have to deal with over the next few days. No big deal—you know, just rain, snow, cold, and scattered tornados.

Hmmmm.

This morning, like every morning, I walked out of the hotel to see legs coming out from under *Something*. It was just Dave, up early and performing his morning maintenance routine. A little tweak to the water pump bushing, a little squirt of high-tech lubricant on a critical component, a topping off of oil in the crankcase.

Our plan was to make it to Wyoming that day. With a potential snowstorm heading in our direction, we wanted to go as far west as possible before it and *Something* collided, possibly in Utah.

Right then, though, on the morning of our tenth day on the road, there was not a cloud in sight. In fact, it might have been the most beautiful morning of our trip so far.

3. Heading toward Nebraska's western border, the scenery got more beautiful with every mile. When the word "prairie" was invented, this is what they had in mind: grassy meadows with cattle grazing as far as I could see. And we were now driving through quite a bit of elevation, as opposed to the flat eastern side of the state.

Rolling hills and smooth pavement made for a memorable drive.

You could almost set the cruise control and take a nap. These roads through America's heartland are straight as an arrow. And beautiful. The huge farms on both sides of the road go off, seemingly, forever.

4. We were rapidly approaching the intersection where we had to make the most critical decision of our trip: Colorado or Wyoming?

The Lincoln Highway splits, so both routes are "correct." The southern route heads through Denver, then goes west over the Eisenhower Pass through a fairly severe section of the Rocky Mountains. The northern Lincoln Highway route continues due west through the Nebraska panhandle and into Wyoming.

The mountains on this route are supposedly less serious than through Colorado.

So, what's the downside with Wyoming? Basically, the Lincoln Highway, still Highway 30 at this point, disappears, making I-80 the only east–west route. The legal speed limit in Wyoming is as high as 80 miles per hour, meaning *Something* would be driving as much as 25 or 30 miles per hour slower than the prevailing traffic.

Concerning.

But then there was the impending winter storm, which would likely be more intense in higher elevations of Colorado than further north in Wyoming.

Dave, Michael, and I discussed it and decided to remain on the northern route through Wyoming—making the climb up Colorado's steep mountain grades would be laborious for *Something*, especially if we had to do it in the snow. This we all wanted to avoid.

5. When I was a kid, every gas station had service bays. It was there you would bring your car for a tune-up, oil change, brakes, or new tires. The

Fuel:
116.57 GALLONS
Distance:
2,168 MILES

The permanence of these grain silos provide an interesting backdrop to our speedy little Model T, zipping past them at a nice 50-ish mile-per-hour clip.

mechanics knew their trade, and customers received quality service for less money than dealerships charged.

Dave's own dad owned a Sinclair service station just like this. "My father would perform all general service short of rebuilding an engine," he said.

But as car companies, probably by design, started producing cars that were too complicated, it became harder for the average country mechanic to repair them. Dealerships make lots of money on service, sometimes more profit than on the sale of the actual car. These days, special training and computers are required, so a self-taught mechanic with a box of wrenches can no longer make a living at the gas station.

About thirty years ago, stations began converting their service bays into convenience stores. Suddenly it became much less likely for a motorist to run down to the station for a tire balance than for a gallon of milk—or just a place to take a leak.

To observe the decline of the American service station, one must simply observe the line of people waiting to use the restrooms. Though they're provided as a convenience for fueling customers, now plenty of noncustomers stop in just to use the facilities. And, admittedly, that includes this cross-country Model T crew.

American gas stations: the official place to take a leak. It's a sad commentary.

That's why it was nostalgic to see a service station in Chappell, Nebraska, with three service bays. Mechanics there performed service work like in the good old days. And fuel was offered in three grades: 87 octane with 10 percent ethanol, 89 octane with 5 percent ethanol, and 91 octane with 0 percent ethanol. Most of the stations we'd seen in the rural Midwest the past few days had offered only one choice, 87 with ethanol, which probably makes sense because ethanol is made from corn, which mostly comes from the Midwest.

After running out of gas a couple of times, thankfully within a stone's throw from a station, we decided to stop every three hours to fill up. That formula worked as long as we remembered to look at our watches . . .

6. Some of the towns we drove through, like Sidney, Nebraska, seemed vibrant and had thriving downtowns with motels, restaurants, and car dealerships. Sadly, other towns, such as Lodgepole, just 19 miles west of Sidney, had business districts without businesses.

Some of these towns were close enough to I-80 that the interstate was within sight of Main Street. When these federally funded, limited-access highways were completed, most of the mom-and-pop-run businesses that catered to east–west travelers dried up and disappeared. Between Walmarts and the interstate franchise restaurants and hotel chains, it's a wonder there are any small towns remaining at all.

7. It had been a productive morning; we'd left Ogallala at about 8:30 and made it to the Wyoming state line before lunch. It was a pleasant 131-mile drive.

In a modern car, I would love to see an 80-mile-per-hour speed limit sign, but in *Something*, I had some concerns. We could cruise all day at 55 miles per hour, truly enjoying the ride, but when the rest of traffic is moving at 80—and faster, since we all know that motorists tend to drive 10 miles per hour or more over the speed limit—they could be passing us at nearly twice our speed.

Several weeks earlier I had called the Montana Highway Patrol. I told them we would be driving a slower-than-average vehicle on I-80 and asked for their advice; the trooper put me on hold for a few minutes, then returned to the phone.

"We don't have any minimum speeds on our highways, but if you were going 25 or 30 miles per hour, I'd recommend another route," she said. When I told her we'd be going 50 to 55, she didn't seem concerned.

"I think you'll be alright,"

It was this concern for safety, however, that led us to install the orange bicycle flag on a 6-foot fiberglass pole onto *Something*'s back bumper, plus a third brake light and emergency flashers. All worthy modifications, I think. And Michael would be behind us driving the Escape with the emergency flashers on.

So I didn't feel as intimidated anymore about driving the 400-plus miles across Wyoming. I couldn't, because there were no alternatives that didn't involve going hundreds of miles out of our way. We decided to go for it.

In fact, I thought, this might be a blessing after all. We were driving directly into a predicted storm coming from the west, and if we were still traveling on the more traditional Lincoln Highway, we would slowly approach the weather. But on I-80, we'd be rapidly driving toward the storm, and in my Type A personality logic, that meant we'd be able to get through it quicker.

Anyway, that's how I justified it as the first few raindrops just hit the windshield. A preview of things to come.

8. Crossing into Wyoming, we had just entered our tenth state. Once we traversed these 427 miles, we'd only have three states remaining: Utah, Nevada, and California.

We were approaching the three-quarters completed mark.

In preparation for this trip, I read of number of travel books: John Steinbeck's *Travels with Charley*, Bill Bryson's *The Lost Continent* and *A Walk*

in the Woods, William Least Heat-Moon's *Blue Highways*, and a few others. I wanted to get myself in the right state of mind for documenting this adventure. In most of the books I read, though, it became evident to me that the writer was becoming bored or fatigued with the journey by the book's three-quarter mark, quickly trying to bring the story to a conclusion. As a reader, this was my own impression, and may not have actually been the case.

But I'm very conscious of this tendency, so I am promising you, the reader, that I will do my best to keep the story alive as I continue to take you for a ride in our rumble seat.

9. When we set out on the morning of Day 10, the sky was 100 percent blue. Just beautiful. But as we continued westward, more clouds began to come from the western horizon. While still in Nebraska, west of Ogallala, the ratio of sun to clouds had been 50:50. Now as we crossed into eastern Wyoming, the ratio favored the clouds by 80:20.

And it had gotten colder.

That morning, Dave and I started off in T-shirts and shorts, but, as the day progressed, found ourselves donning long-sleeved shirts and jackets. We kept the shorts, but it was getting chilly.

10. We decided to make a run for it. We were about 250 miles from Rock Springs, which appeared on my atlas to be just on the other side of the mountains.

We had already covered about 150 miles, so another 250 would make a record-mileage day for *Something*. But if we could make it through the Rockies, especially with the potential snow, I knew we'd be thankful.

· ·

11. "Nobody goes to McDonald's because they want to," my friend and former coworker Mel Poole once espoused to me when we were looking for a quick meal during a trip to the Daytona 500.

I couldn't argue with him. Unlike when I was a kid, when a trip to McDonald's was a fun family experience, as an adult it has sadly become a place to eat only when there is no alternative.

So, thank goodness for McDonald's. We stopped in for a quick lunch and were back on the road in no time, racing that storm. Well, not before Dave changed into long pants between cars in the parking lot when nobody was looking.

My phone's weather app told me there was a high probability of thundershowers and a likelihood of snow for the next couple of days. That would put a real damper (pardon the pun) on our western trek. *Something* was not equipped with snow tires, a heater, or even roll-up windows. The doors have snap-in canvas and plastic side curtains that we had not yet installed—but even if we did, cold and moisture would still likely penetrate the cockpit.

In my suitcase I had packed an outer-shell jacket with a hood, a sweatshirt, a couple of long-sleeved shirts, and a wool beanie cap, so I thought I'd be in pretty good shape. Plus I had brought a pair of gloves my father had given to me probably thirty years before. They are not looking so good these days, with holes in a couple of the fingers, but I refuse to replace them—they are about the only things I have left from him. But packing for a trip like this means traveling light, and that means leaving lots of clothing items at home.

Dave seemed to be equally well prepared, and Michael—yes, Michael was enjoying his drive in the 2017 Ford Escape, equipped not only with heat and windows but with heated seats.

Over lunch, I kidded Michael that he could simulate our ride in *Something* by turning on the air conditioning and opening the windows. He pretended not to hear me.

Fuel:
117.57 GALLON
Distance:
2,338 MILES
· · · · · · · · ·

· ·

12. Oops . . . we did it again, with all due respect to Britney Spears. For the third time on this trip, we had run out of fuel. And for the first time, it was not in front of a gas station—we were on I-80, about 10 miles from Laramie. We rationalized that because we were traveling at top speed, almost 60 miles per hour, into a strong headwind, we had used significantly more fuel than on previous days.

Luckily, a few days earlier Dave had found an old 1-gallon windshield-washer fluid container, which he'd filled with gas and stored in the trunk just in case. Disaster circumvented, or at least delayed. But we'd installed that

OPPOSITE: When the temperature started dropping in Wyoming, long pants, jackets, gloves, and hats were put on. And the side curtains were installed on *Something*'s doors, right on the side of the road, if necessary.

gallon of gas about 10 miles before, and we had been getting about 18 miles per gallon on the open road. We would have soon been running on fumes again if it hadn't been for the oasis called Laramie.

Again we added 10.5 gallons into the 10-gallon fuel cell, meaning we were within moments, probably 2 miles, of running out again. While we were at the gas pumps, a little girl ran over to our car. Her father soon joined her.

Fuel:
128.07 GALLONS
Distance:
2,354 MILES
··········

"Is it OK if my daughter sits in your car for a minute?" he asked. "I told her she probably won't see another one like it."

She introduced herself as Riley. Her father, Dane, told us that she really likes mechanical things.

"She races in motocross," he said.

"And I'm starting in go karts," Riley added.

Riley told me she was nine years old and in third grade.

"But there are only twelve and a half days left until school is over."

But who's counting?

Before we began our journey, Dave had had a couple of dozen children's T-shirts made as souvenirs in the event we'd meet a kid just like Riley. They had *Ford Model T Coast to Coast* and the names of the three of us. It was a great idea—we had been giving them away little by little, and we still had a pink one in Riley's size.

While we were stopped for fuel, we decided to take the opportunity to install the side curtains. These are canvas and clear plastic affairs, much like a speedboat might have. For early roadsters like *Something*, they were what passed for weather gear.

And it must be said that once we were back on the road, the change in *Something*'s interior was instantly noticeable. The cockpit was almost toasty in comparison to just a few minutes earlier. The temperature had dropped some 20 degrees, from 65 degrees in the morning to 45 degrees at our fuel stop.

These side curtains could prove to be our saving grace.

Seeing that we were concerned about the weather, Riley's dad Dane told us the storm was due to hit the following day, Wednesday, and recommended that we try to make it over the mountains and into Rock Springs that night.

"This way you can be on your way to Salt Lake City tomorrow," he said. "Maybe the storm will go north from there."

We thanked Dane for the weather tip and wished Riley good luck on her budding racing career. Danica Patrick, you better watch out!

We were soon back on westbound I-80 with undoubtedly more adventures ahead. I just hoped running out of gas again wouldn't be one of them.

13. The temperature had risen to about 50 degrees, and between Dave and me putting on heavier clothing and installing the side curtains, it had gotten positively balmy in the cockpit. The sun would occasionally sneak out for a moment now and then, so it seemed our worries of a storm were over for the time being.

Then we passed an electronic billboard displaying a weather report. It warned us of an impending snowstorm from 11:00 p.m. that night until 9:00 a.m. Friday.

We'd have to keep the pedal to the metal if we were going to stand a chance of getting out of Dodge before the snowflakes fell.

14. Wyoming's terrain is vastly different from Nebraska's. First, we were about 7,500 feet above sea level, up from Nebraska's sub-1,500. Then, the terrain has quite a bit of elevation change, giving us rolling hills and occasionally exposed rock. The mountains in the distance had snow-covered peaks.

The scenery had all the makings of a pretty postcard or a watercolor painting.

We were extremely lucky, because at the moment we were being bathed in warm sunlight, and the temperature had risen a bit further to 55 degrees. I apologize for mentioning the weather so often, but when you're riding in a minimalist car, the weather—temperature, wind, clouds, rain—becomes a constant traveling companion. It's hard to escape the constant physical sensations that change every time a cloud covers the sun.

To the north I saw dark clouds and rain, but for the time being, we were sitting pretty.

15. I had to admit that I missed the slower pace of the traditional Lincoln Highway—of Highway 30, on which we had traveled pretty much since Philadelphia, with its 50-mile-per-hour speed limits, old buildings, and occasional points of interest.

I was told the state of Wyoming did not have the finances to construct the new I-80 to run alongside the Lincoln Highway, so it just absorbed Highway 30 into the high-speed interstate throughout the entire state. So, all things considered, if we had to scoot through the state in order to beat the impending storm, I guess we benefitted from I-80.

BELOW: The littlest enthusiast. Budding motocross and go-kart racer Riley Smith checked out our car. Her dad, Dane, said his nine-year-old daughter has a talent for driving fast, and loves everything mechanical.

Red sky at night, sailor's delight . . . except if you are driving through rural Wyoming. This dramatic sunset was a sign that the weather was about to make a drastic change.

16. As we drove, I tried to book rooms for us at the Hampton Inn in Rock Springs, which would be the first large town on the other side of the Rockies. But my attempt at online reservations told me that no rooms were available. Same with Homewood Suites, another Hilton property.

So I decided to call on the phone to see if I could sweet-talk my way into a couple of rooms. Well, I'm sure you can guess what happened next: I was transferred to customer service and was speaking with a Hilton customer service rep in India! Now, remember that I am riding in a Model T at 55 miles per hour with fabric side curtains and a convertible top. And I'm talking to a gentleman who I'm sure was very nice, but who is on the other side of the world and doesn't have a 100 percent handle on the English language.

I realized he was probably required to go through a set series of questions, but my patience was running short.

"No, I don't need a rental car, and I know there is free breakfast from 6:00 to 9:00 a.m. in the lobby and there are an exercise room and pool available for my pleasure," I said. "But I just need two hotel rooms before I lose cell-phone coverage!"

What resulted was a confusing twenty-minute phone conversation as we tried to communicate around the globe. Two men separated by a common language.

And I'm sure you can guess what happened next . . . I lost the connection.

Fuel:
132.97 GALLONS
Distance:
2,439 MILES
. . . .

17. After driving for a couple of hours through the Wyoming mountains, I was pretty convinced that the morning's forecast of 40-plus-mile-per-hour wind gusts had been accurate. I fought the steering wheel left and right, especially through areas with sheer cliffs on both sides of the road, which created a wind-tunnel effect.

When cell-phone coverage returned, I tried again to book hotel rooms in Rock Springs, but still no luck. It seemed the threat of a snow storm had people hunkering down early.

But we lucked out with a hotel in Green River, 15 miles west of Rock Springs. It was a Hampton Inn at the foot of a mountain with beautiful rock formations that were lit up with spotlights when we arrived at 10:00 p.m.

Fuel:
141.31 GALLONS
Distance:
2,569 MILES

18. This was the first time Dave and I had words. It was bound to happen—I mean, we'd spent ten days less than 1 inch apart from each other since we'd left New York.

When I woke up on Wednesday morning and went downstairs for breakfast, light snow was falling. And the wind was blowing very hard, 40- to 50-mile-per-hour gusts. And it was 28 degrees.

"We're not going anywhere today," Dave said. He had probably already been up for hours, servicing *Something* and making plans. "I'm worried about our safety."

"What do you mean?" I asked. "The really bad weather is moving in tonight. If we don't get out of here quickly, we could be snowed in for days."

Dave walked one way and I walked the other, each of us trying to avoid a verbal confrontation in front of other guests and the hotel staff. After all, we still had to sit next to each other for at least five more days.

After some more "words" from both of us, we decided to take a test drive on I-80 to see if *Something* was up to the task. We'd see how bad the roads were and how fierce the headwinds were blowing. The road surface was wet, but not yet icy. But the wind was horrible—as we traveled west, trying to attain a speed of 50 miles an hour in a 40-mile-per-hour headwind, we had the equivalent of a 90-mile-per-hour torrent blowing across the car. Much of it came into the cockpit, despite having the side curtains installed.

More fabulous Wyoming landscape.

Dave was adamant that we'd stay in Green River one more night. I was adamant that we'd depart and attempt to beat the bad weather. Dave was predicting that the cold and wind would be too much for him to bear.

"Who's going to be colder, Dave, you or me?" I asked. "I'm not going to ride in the Escape. I'm riding in the T, right next to you."

We shook hands and decided to make the call at 11:00 a.m., the hotel checkout time. It was only 8:00, so we had three hours to kill.

Michael went to the room to edit photos and send them to his remote server. I worked on notes for this book, and Dave fiddled on the car, mostly the side curtains, which had too many air gaps for this type of weather. Using a roll of electrical wire he had in the trunk, he was able to fit them much tighter.

While waiting for our hopeful departure time, we happily told other guests in the Hampton Inn lobby about our adventure, explaining that we were actually heading toward San Francisco.

"Oh, that cute little car shouldn't be out in the snow and cold," one woman told us as she was checking out of the hotel. "It should be at home in a warm garage."

I was going to add, "Along with its occupants," but decided not to.

At 11:00 a.m., we all decided to leave, determined to make it to Salt Lake City, 200 miles away, by dusk. Michael had already secured hotel rooms there for that evening.

As was often the case after heavy rains, when the Lincoln Highway turned to a sticky mud called "gumbo," cars had to be pulled free by horses. *Lincoln Highway Digital Image Collection, University of Michigan Library (Special Collections Library)*

I must admit that waiting those three hours made sense. I-80 was now dry, the outside temperature had warmed into the mid-30s, and the partially blue skies to the west now gave us the promise of sunshine.

And Dave and I were still friends.

But I was the manager of the budget on the trip, which required not spending unnecessary money for hotel rooms we didn't need.

The wind was still pretty fierce, but *Something* seemed up to the task. It was amazing to me that this old car was driving much faster than it was designed to, but yet, like a Timex watch, it just kept ticking. And those ninety-two-year-old Babbitt bearings were still spinning away at much higher RPMs than old Henry Ford ever imagined. Knock on lead.

An early Lincoln Highway motorist is driving his car nearly up to its axles in rural Utah. *Lincoln Highway Digital Image Collection, University of Michigan Library (Special Collections Library)*

I was the passenger for the morning's windy drive, and I used the time to take some more notes. I had been writing notes from time to time on bumpy roads for the past week and a half, and it had been a challenge, but writing with gloves on proved to be even more so. I only hoped that when I referred back to these notes in two months, I could read them!

19. Before leaving that morning, Dave had performed his morning ritual of servicing the car, topping off the fluids, lubing the suspension and valves. We had also gone to a corner of the hotel parking lot and drained the radiator—it had been filled with pure water, but with these subfreezing temperatures, we didn't want to chance cracking *Something*'s engine block.

We had purchased 3 gallons of premixed antifreeze during our last fuel stop, 2 of which would be used to fill the radiator and 1 of which would be a spare. *Something* still liked to mark her territory wherever we parked, so in addition to oil, we also needed to top off the radiator every once in a while.

20. The woman behind the front desk at our hotel had warned us about the road to the west.

"Before you get to the Utah border and Salt Lake City, you'll have to deal with the Three Sisters," she said.

I shook with terror. Suddenly I felt that we were about to face a huge challenge before we could gain passage to the Palace of Salt.

I imagined confronting a killer rabbit or an armless soldier who would boast of only having a flesh wound, as in *Monty Python and the Holy Grail*. Or perhaps our car would be chased down a stone corridor by a boulder like in *Raiders of the Lost Ark*.

"But milord, we only seek passage into your kingdom in order to secure a night's lodging at the Super 8 Motel," I imagined myself saying as we begged for our lives.

Whoops, just a daydream.

"The Three Sisters are pretty steep, rolling hills," the woman continued. "We only put sand on roads here in Wyoming, but they salt roads in Utah, so you should be OK if it snowed there overnight."

As we drove toward the Three Sisters on I-80, I saw some pretty treacherous snow-covered mountains to the left. I surmised that those were the Colorado Rockies, which were about 20 miles to the south.

I was confident we'd made the right decision in going through Wyoming rather than Colorado. Whatever precipitation and wind we were experiencing that morning, I was sure it would be much worse to the south. Plus, the pass through the Rockies was so much higher and steeper than in Wyoming—I'd hate to be crossing on I-70 west of Denver on a morning that.

21. The headwind we were driving into was incredible. It reminded me of a story my friend Peter Egan had told me as we drove my Cobra cross-country from San Francisco to Charlotte.

Peter and his wife, Barb, once flew their Piper Cub from Los Angeles to Virginia to visit friends during a summer vacation. They had planned to spend most of the summer exploring the United States in their light aircraft.

Peter told me that pilots of light planes who decide to fly cross-country always wrestle with the dilemma of how to cross the Rocky Mountains. The elevation of flying over the range is a challenge, and the winds can be pretty fierce.

"One day we landed at a small airport in Colorado and spent the night," Peter told me. "When we woke up in the morning, a pretty strong wind was blowing out of the east. So we took off into the wind and planned to find an altitude where the wind would allow us to make up some ground to the east.

"But we fought those strong headwinds all day, regardless of altitude. We flew backwards at times, and were lucky to make it back to the same airport we started at that morning."

Peter's Piper Cub adventure was one of the inspirations I had when dreaming about taking this trip one day. I didn't think *Something* would be blown backward toward the town of Green River, but I did wish the winds were blowing at our tail rather than into our windshield for a change.

Another person who inspired me to take this trip was Cris Sommer Simmons. I became friends with Cris several years ago when I coauthored a book with Ken Gross and Michael Alan Ross called *Rockin' Garages*, which featured rock-and-roll musicians whose offstage passion is cars and motorcycles.

Cris's husband, Pat Simmons, whom not surprisingly she met at the Sturgis Motorcycle Rally, is the lead guitarist and cofounder of the Doobie Brothers. The book featured the couple, who both share a passion for finding, restoring, and riding vintage motorcycles.

When we met at a concert in Orlando, Cris was getting ready to participate in a reenactment of the Cannonball Baker coast-to-coast endurance run, which pays tribute to Erwin "Cannonball" Baker. Baker made at least 143 record-setting cross-country runs on bikes and in cars. The modern re-creation attempts to duplicate his 1914 run, when he traversed the country in eleven days, twelve hours, and ten minutes on an Indian motorcycle.

If this photo were in black and white, it could have been taken a hundred years ago, when the Lincoln Highway was mostly surfaced in dirt and gravel.

In 2010, Cris, along with 124 other riders, left Kitty Hawk, North Carolina, and arrived in Los Angeles seventeen days later. Here's the catch: only motorcycles built before 1915 were eligible. Cris kept a detailed diary of the trip for her book, documenting the months of preparation, then the day-to-day grind of riding across the country slowly.

For instance, she recounts an episode on Day 2 while she was riding from Kitty Hawk to Greenville, North Carolina:

> One thing I found out today is that the rear cylinder on this bike gets very hot. My right calf feels like it is sunburned and red when I take my boots off. Ouch! I will try to figure a way to wrap something on it for tomorrow. I get back to my room, totally exhausted, with my clothes full of oil and sweat. I finally take my boot off to inspect my swollen foot. I jump into a cool shower and I'll admit . . . I finally let my tears flow. My husband calls and I think I must have been pretty upset. He tells me that I don't need to do this. . . I don't have to prove anything to anyone and that it's okay to quit. Quit? I tell him . . . No way . . . I've come too far . . . I can do this! There is no way I want to quit. My foot is fine and tomorrow is another day. A 225-mile day to be exact. I hope I can sleep!

Because the Lincoln Highway is Interstate 80 in Wyoming, this is what we saw for a couple of days. No old buildings and no friendly people to talk with, just hundreds of miles of 80-miles-per-hour interstate highway being driven at 56 miles per hour.

I followed the progress of Cris and her all-girl pit crew on the Internet as she rode 3,325 miles across the United States on the 1915 Harley-Davidson called *Effie*. The bike was named after Effie Hotchkiss, who rode a motorcycle cross-country in 1915. Oh, and Effie's mother, Avis, rode along in a sidecar.

"Effie's bike was the same make and model as my bike," Cris said. "So I named my bike *Effie* in her honor. She was the first woman to ride a motorcycle cross-country. I wanted to recapture the adventure that Effie and Avis experienced on that trip."

CANNONBALL BAKER

Erwin George "Cannonball" Baker was a larger-than-life American daredevil in the early part of the last century, and is still a cult hero among certain car enthusiasts today. Born in Indiana in 1882, Baker quickly forgot his career in vaudeville acting once he won his first dirt-track motorcycle race in 1904. The hook was set, and Baker spent the rest of his life pursuing speed.

He made nearly 150 cross-country and endurance record runs on various motorcycles for a combined total of approximately 550,000 miles. In 1914, he rode an Indian motorcycle from the East Coast to the West Coast in just eleven days, did a quick about-face, and drove a Stutz Bearcat automobile from west to east in another eleven days.

Baker once left Indianapolis on his Indian Motorcycle and didn't return home until he had completed 14,000 miles, three months later.

The record run that put Baker's name on the map came in 1933, when he drove a Graham-Paige from New York to Los Angeles in just 53.5 hours. That record stood for forty years and became the inspiration for the Cannonball Baker Sea-to-Shining-Sea Memorial Trophy Dash, which was founded by the late automotive journalist Brock Yates.

Baker later became the first commissioner of NASCAR.

Cannonball Baker, who died in 1960, was inducted into the Motorsport Hall of Fame in 1989 and the American Motorcyclist Association Motorcycle Hall of Fame in 1998.

Since that first Cannonball Run, Cris has participated in two more reenactments: one from Daytona Beach, Florida, to Tacoma, Washington, and the other from Atlantic City, New Jersey, to San Diego, California.

"It's never easy," she said. "Even when it has rained for four days straight and it's cold, you still have to force yourself [to get] out of bed and get back on the road. People just love to see these old bikes on the road. They usually only see them in museums."

Husband Pat has participated in two of the events himself, his band's touring schedule always taking priority.

When I started to research the Cannonball, I became excited about the idea of traversing the country on a similar vintage bike. I briefly considered buying an old motorcycle like Cris's, but, not being a serious rider, I felt the long-distance trek might be a big bite for me to chew. That's when I started to consider an old car, specifically a Model T.

When I spoke to Cris while working on this book, she was excited to tell me that she would again be riding *Effie* in the 2018 Cannonball Run, which will begin in Portland, Maine, and end in Portland, Oregon.

"My last trip is always my 'last trip,'" she said. "At the conclusion, I'm always done, tired. But those people are my tribe, my family. So I'll ride cross-country at least one more time."

Her book was one of the inspirations for me to make a similar trip, and now, eight years later, there I was.

In addition to *Cannonball Diary* (2012), Cris Sommer Simmons has authored two other terrific books about motorcycles: a children's book called *Patrick Wants to Ride* (1994) and a history called *The American Motorcycle Girls: 1900 to 1950* (2009). Autographed copies of these books are available from Cris's website, cannonballcris.com.

22. The Three Sisters were challenging, but none of us lost any limbs in the crossing. We achieved our highest elevation to date: 7,400 feet. *Something* trucked up those inclines with aplomb.

Like the Little Engine That Could, our little car went *chug, chug, chug, puff, puff, puff*, but it climbed those Three Sisters without ever shifting into low gear.

I think I can, I think I can—up the steepest Sister at a maintained speed of 41 miles per hour!

23. Welcome to Utah!

About two hours after leaving Green River, Wyoming, we crossed into our eleventh state—and immediately hit snow. I'm talking right at the state line. It's as though Wyoming wouldn't allow snow to enter the state, so it was being held up in Utah. It was a light snow, and the road was fairly dry, but the wind made it look dramatic with white powder blowing around us.

Fabulous million-year-old rock formations make our speedster look young in comparison.

Utah would be a relatively short state to cross, about 250 miles altogether. Our plan was to lodge in Salt Lake City and drive into Nevada tomorrow.

But first we had to make a required stop at the famed Bonneville Salt Flats near Wendover. I've always dreamed of going there for Speed Weeks, which is in August, but this would have to suffice for now. Maybe when we got there we'd put *Something* on the salt to see what she could do. Maybe we'd hit 70!

Same place, a hundred years earlier. This photo was taken at Echo Canyon in Utah, in 1915. *Detroit Public Library Lincoln Highway Digital Archive*

24. Until then, Dave and I would be freezing our tushes off, fighting the cold, drafts, and high winds as Michael followed us in the Escape.

Now, let me reiterate: the Escape had not only heat, but heated seats. Yet Michael was dressed for an artic expedition, with a down-filled vest, heavy winter coat, gloves, and hat. Like it was cold in there or something.

Gee, Michael, I certainly hope the heat doesn't get stuck in the high position or you might get too toasty.

Dressed for winter. When we arrived in Salt Lake City, after a windy day on the road in our cold Model T, we were ready for a hot meal, a hot shower, and a warm bed.

25. It was in Utah that we crossed one of the prettiest scenes of the trip thus far. It was immediately to the south of I-80, to our left. It included horses grazing in a meadow of the greenest grass I have ever seen, with an old wooden barn and weathered fencing in the foreground and the snow-covered Rocky Mountains in the background. It was all captured under a deep blue sky. It was a *National Geographic* cover scene with no color correction required.

Just take my word for it.

They just don't make scenery like that on the East Coast.

It's interesting how each state has its own physical character. Within just a few miles of crossing into Utah, it was immediately obvious that we weren't in Wyoming anymore, Toto. The scenery was dramatic, with steep, rugged mountains and huge rock outcroppings. Some of the lower mountains were brilliant green, obviously fooled into thinking that spring had officially arrived. Snow dominated on the taller peaks in the distance.

It was also in Utah that we experienced our first mechanical malfunction, however minor: a blown fuse rendered our brake lights inoperable. And nonfunctioning brake lights made things stressful for Michael, who was following close behind us with his emergency flashers on.

To remedy this, Dave borrowed the fuse from the *ahooooga* horn and installed it in the brake-fuse holder. We wouldn't be able to blast the distinctive horn at passersby anymore, but we felt functioning brake lights would prove to be the better part of valor.

That's it. *Something* had operated well since we'd departed from Times Square eleven days before, and with any luck, that would continue—knock on wood.

26. The car continued to run well as we approached Salt Lake City, where we would overnight.

It had proven to be a good call to travel today; otherwise we would have wasted a beautiful driving day by watching political-nonsense television in the Green Valley Hampton Inn. And possibly gotten caught up in a snowstorm than could have delayed us and ultimately made our driving even more hazardous.

By the time we got to Salt Lake, with apologies to Glenn Campbell, we would have another 200 miles under our belts. Hopefully we'd arrive early enough to be able to enjoy dinner when the rest of the world enjoys it, and not at 10:00 p.m., as had been our norm.

Fuel:
151.91 GALLONS
Distance:
2,726 MILES

27. It was a wonderful experience being able to pass police and state-trooper speed traps at full speed without experiencing that "pucker" effect after passing, wondering whether you've just got nailed by their radar gun. You know the feeling: when you spend the next five minutes staring in the rearview mirror waiting to see flashing lights behind you?

That's the beauty of driving *Something*, a vehicle not capable of breaking the speed limit almost anywhere.

Me adding more coolant, or in this case, we'll call it antifreeze. Because *Something* doesn't have a closed, pressurized system, and because the engine tolerances are not precise, we had to add fluids every day.

28. We made it to Salt Lake City in time for dinner. After leaving our luggage at the hotel, Michael and I headed to a microbrewery within walking distance that the nice lady behind the hotel's desk recommended.

On the way, we passed by a Barnes & Noble book store. We stopped inside to look at the car magazines, because, for the time being, Barnes & Noble still has the best selection around. But I must admit that one of the greatest thrills as an author is to walk into a book store that has a hundred thousand books on the shelves and find one of mine on the shelf amongst them! Michael and I found our way to the transportation section, which is becoming smaller and increasingly difficult to locate—it's usually next to the bathroom door or beside the children's puzzles.

We found two copies of a book that Michael and I had done together a couple of years ago, *Route 66 Barn Find Road Trip*. I also located copies of some other books I had written, *The Hemi in the Barn* and *The Harley in the Barn*. I asked the gentleman behind the counter, Mike Minoughan, if he'd like us to sign the store's copies.

"Oh, yeah, that would be great," he said.

As Michael and I were signing, Mike told us he was a car guy too. Car people are everywhere, even in unlikely spots like bookstores.

"I was born in Toronto, but when I was ten, my family moved to Ohio," he said. "We needed a new car, so my mom sent my father to the Ford dealer to buy a Country Squire station wagon, but he came home with a 1969 Mustang fastback with a 351-cubic-inch engine and a four-speed instead. One night my father was driving too fast and tried to outrun the cops. He got caught, but thankfully they were very nice to him.

"Later my dad got into MGs. We had them all over the place—it got to the point that my mother couldn't park her car in the garage because of the MG engines all over the floor."

So how did Mike wind up in Salt Lake City?

"A woman brought me here twenty years ago," he said. "Now we've got two kids. There is such great access to the outdoors. Utah is the most beautiful state I've ever been to. I love the people and the lack of population. There is also a lack of attitude here that I so enjoy."

The car-guy genes have apparently been transferred to a third Minoughan generation.

Much of the Lincoln Highway was built adjacent to railroad tracks because they were always on gentle grades. Passing a freight train in Nevada must have been typical of what travelers experienced in the early days of Lincoln Highway motoring.

"My son Max is really into Impalas," Mike said. "He gets his driver's license this month."

Mike told us that he truly enjoys working in a bookstore. He was once the store manager, but told us that he now enjoys a less responsible position as assistant manager.

"It's really a blessing," he said. "I had cancer and I couldn't work for a year. Doctors had to remove my large intestine. I had operations and chemo. "My wife travels in her job, so a few extra hours mean that I can be the parent always at home."

Now, on to the microbrewery: there was a pale ale with my name on it waiting for me.

29. The morning was cold, 36 degrees, but at least there was no wind. It was also partly sunny, which made all the difference when compared to our hotel departure just twenty-four hours earlier.

The forecast was for temperatures to rise into the mid-50s with heavier clouds moving in later in the morning. The sky above Salt Lake City was crystal blue as we drove out of town, westbound on I-80, dotted with cotton-puffy white clouds here and there. The sun was playing hide-and-

Same location? We saw this photo in the archives and wondered if it was taken in a similar place as the photo Michael took with *Something* passing a train on the right. *Library of Congress*

seek every few minutes, as Dave and I could easily feel. The temperatures dropped noticeably every time the sun hid behind a cloud.

The city skyline looked steel and modern, probably recently constructed. But always in the background were the sharp, knife-edge mountains that took nature millions of years to build. An interesting juxtaposition.

Closer to home, the inside cockpit temperature was 40 degrees, according to the Automobile Thermometer, Made In USA accessory gauge that was mounted on the dashboard, possibly for the past ninety years or so.

Fuel:
158.24 GALLONS
Distance:
2,821 MILES

Our destination that morning was the Bonneville Salt Flats at the Utah–Nevada state line. Michael absolutely raves about the place—he has attended Speed Weeks there seven times as a team photographer for a group of guys who compete in a 1932 Ford roadster.

"Maybe we can grab lunch at the Salt Flats Café," he said as we left the parking lot at the Extended Stay hotel.

We tooled along the highway at a comfortable 55 miles per hour, 4,212 feet above sea level. The windshield and side curtains blocked much of the cold wind. Then a BMW 1200 GS motorcycle, decked out with all the saddlebags and accessories, passed us doing probably 70 or 75.

That guy must be tough, I thought. But then again, he likely had on an electrically heated one-piece suit and heated handlebar controls.

I had calculated that we didn't need fuel yet, but Michael warned us that there were no gas stations between there and Wendover, about 100 miles away. So 6.3 gallons filled us up.

Good call, Mikey.

30. I had never seen the salt lake in Salt Lake City before. At least not in person. I had seen photos of it in *National Geographic* magazine as a child. I was in Nokomis Elementary School and was impressed to see the photo of a man seemingly able to float on top of the water without effort because of the lake's high salinity.

And now we were passing that same lake immediately to our right. It's a fairly massive stretch from there all the way over to the base of the distant mountains. With no point of reference, it was hard to tell where the lake ended and the mountains and the sky began—it could have been 30 miles away or 10 miles away.

We passed a Morton's salt refinery on the right, located right on the lake. A company like Morton's should have a long supply of salt at a location like that. No wonder the lady back at our hotel in Green River said Utah salts its roads; it's all over the place!

31. What can be said about driving through Utah on I-80? It's flat, nonagricultural land, with just scrub brush as far as the eye can see— except, of course, for the mountains in the distance in every direction.

Some of these mountains are lower and more rounded; I wondered whether these are the older ones. The taller, sharper ones like we saw earlier are probably the youngsters, only tens of millions of years old, rather than hundreds of millions.

Some mountains had snow on their peaks, which seemed to attract clouds on this otherwise cloudless day. I remember a similar effect when my son Brian and I were camping in Denali National Park a dozen years ago—on a beautiful, sunny day, Denali was shrouded in clouds, the result of condensation caused by the cold snow meeting the air warmed by the sun.

Out there, between Salt Lake City and Wendover, I hadn't seen a house or even a building for a long time. This would be a lonely place to break down in the middle of the night, and I was very thankful Michael had advised us to purchase fuel that morning.

The road, I-80, is impossibly straight. I couldn't see a single curve ahead in the west, and I couldn't remember passing any curves during the past hour. There can be no greater contrast on a Lincoln Highway trip than the long, flat, desolate roads of Utah versus the lush, twisty mountain roads of Pennsylvania we'd driven through on the first day of the trip. Yet we were on the same road.

A group of motorcycles came at us from the opposite direction, probably heading toward Salt Lake City. I counted fifty-nine of them and wondered where they were going.

MORTON SALT PLANT

Driving west from Salt Lake City on I-80, it's impossible to ignore the Morton Salt Plant in Grantsville, Utah. The huge plant can be seen for miles in all directions and sits on the Great Salt Lake. At 1,699 square miles, the lake is the largest salt lake in the Western Hemisphere and the eighth largest in the world. Morton harvests salt brine from 1,500 acres of salt lake adjacent to the plant.

The site has been used for salt production since 1912. Morton, which purchased the site in 1991, utilizes evaporation ponds for the production of salt products, including for human and livestock consumption, water softening, and deicing processes. Morton uses the solar salt method of salt production, which means the sun heats up and evaporates the water covering the salt in shallow ponds, leaving a salty brine, which is harvested with machines, cleansed, and processed.

Morton, which has been in business since 1848, employs 130 people in the Grantsville plant. Morton's logo, the Morton Salt Girl, has been used as the company's trademark for more than a hundred years.

Think about that next time you sprinkle salt on your steak or order some salted-caramel ice cream.

THE MECHANICS OF MIRAGES

The textbook definition of a mirage is an optical illusion caused by atmospheric conditions, especially the appearance of a sheet of water in a desert or on a hot road caused by the refraction of light from the sky by heated air.

There are several types of mirages: inferior mirages, superior mirages, heat haze, and Fata Morgana. Without getting into the complexities of each (which I don't understand anyway), the mirages we encountered outside of Salt Lake City were of the inferior variety. These are the ones that confused exhausted early travelers with the image of a lake in the distance. They are referred to as *inferior* because the image is cast below the actual object—in this case, the "object" being the sky. The mirage causes the viewer to see a bright, bluish patch in the distance.

The science behind mirages is that light rays coming from a particular distant object all travel through nearly the same air layers and all are bent over about the same amount. Therefore, rays coming from the top of the object will arrive lower than those from the bottom. The image usually is upside down, enhancing the illusion that the sky image seen in the distance is really a water or oil puddle acting as a mirror.

32. Out there I could see how early settlers, those lost and parched, could be fooled into thinking there was water nearby. There were constant mirages.

They're truly amazing, these images that appear to be an unreachable body of water. Cars coming from the opposite direction even cast reflections into the imaginary "lakes."

Far out.

33. We stopped at a rest area along a salt lake so Dave could lubricate the car.

"We've been driving it so hard for these past 100 miles," he said. "We just need to give it some oil."

But in this rest area, suddenly Dave and *Something* became media stars to a busload of Japanese tourists.

They didn't know much English, but they knew what kind of car it was.

"Model T."

"Model T!"

"Model T," said just about every person in attendance.

Dave posed for probably a hundred photos for his fans. These people loved the car and tried to ask Dave questions in broken English.

"Thank you. One more, please."

After a forty-five-minute photo session, we were ready to leave. But we were prevented because each person then wanted their own photo taken next to the car.

It was a lengthy but enjoyable pit stop.

34. As we pulled into the parking area for the Bonneville Salt Flats in Wendover, we saw a compact car that was stuck about 100 feet out in the wet, briny salt slush. There were a few young people milling about, filthy and trying to push the car out. No luck, though; it was sitting on the chassis, its wheels spinning in salty puddles.

We didn't pay much attention, and took photos of *Something* on the salt at the end of the parking area. There were interesting informational plaques we read about the salt flats' history, and I asked Michael questions about Speed Weeks.

"See that mountain out there?" Michael asked, pointing to a large peak that appeared to be 5 or 10 miles away. "Distance is deceptive out here. All the streamliners steer toward that mountain when they try to break the speed records. It's probably 30 miles from here."

FOLLOWING PAGES: We had arrived at the Holy Land of Speed, the Bonneville Salt Flats. I had dreamed about coming here since I was a kid. Unfortunately we were about two months too early for the record-setting runs. Hopefully someday.

BELOW: Dave and *Something* became minor celebrities at a rest stop adjacent to the Bonneville Salt Flats near Wendover, Nevada. A busload of Japanese tourists each wanted their picture taken with Dave and the Model T.

BONNEVILLE SALT FLATS

We've just driven past the Great Salt Lake, the largest of its kind in the Western Hemisphere. But the largest of the many salt lakes to the west of Great Salt Lake is the remnants of Lake Bonneville, public lands managed by the Bureau of Land Management (BLM), near Wendover, Utah. Bonneville is free and open for the public to drive on, if they like. Or can. It is also the site of Bonneville Speedway, where speed record runs have been attempted since 1914.

Despite concerns that the salt surface has thinned over the years, the BLM conducted comprehensive tests in 2006 and determined that it had not deteriorated appreciably between 1988 to 2003. That was good news for racers. The water that sits on the surface in the winter and spring evaporates in the summer heat, revealing the dense, hard racing surface.

There are five motorsport events that take place on Bonneville Speedway, with the largest, Speed Week, hosted over a six-day period in mid-August. The Southern California Timing Association and the Utah Salt Flats Racing Association host motorcycle, car, and truck speed events. Entrants come from all over the world to compete in hot rods, belly tankers, lakesters, streamliners, motorcycles, and all sorts of trucks as they "shoot the salt" in attempts to break existing speed records in numerous classes. To date, the highest speed achieved by jet- and rocket-propulsion vehicles on the Bonneville Salt Flats was set by Gary Gabelich in October 1970. His *Blue Flame* racing vehicle reached 622.407 miles per hour.

The salt flats were highlighted in the 2005 feature film *The World's Fastest Indian*, which starred Anthony Hopkins and told the story of New Zealand motorcycle racer Burt Munroe and his vintage yet highly modified Indian motorcycle. Competing in a class for two-wheel vehicles, Munroe achieved a speed of 201.851 miles per hour, setting a new record.

I was shocked. I couldn't imagine speed-record cars, which travel up to 600 miles per hour, would aim toward a solid object like that. But then, it really didn't look like it was 30 miles from where we were standing either. After we'd spent about forty-five minutes in the parking lot, taking photos and getting ready to leave, we decided to ask that group of teens with the stuck car if they'd like a hand. Walking toward them, I realized they were standing in a yucky mess—not one that I wished to enter. No way was I walking out there.

But I made them an offer.

"Our Ford Escape over there has four-wheel drive," I said. "We have a tow rope and we can try to pull you out."

"We'd really appreciate it," said a nice girl, Kayla, who seemed to be in charge. She offered to crawl under her car (in the salty mud) and hook up the rope. But it was not long enough.

"No problem," Kayla said. "We have some friends in another car who went out to buy a tow rope. They should be back in a little while."

OPPOSITE TOP: Seems that a carload of high school kids tried to drive their Toyota onto the wet salt flats. When the flats are flooded, they have the consistency of gooey, salty mud. This car was sunk to its axles.

BOTTOM LEFT AND RIGHT: That mountain behind Dave (right) and me is supposedly 30 miles away! It's amazing how deceiving distance can be out here.

High school junior Kayla Banas was the one who volunteered her Toyota to drive fellow film studies students onto the flats to shoot a video. She had tried to dig the car out herself, but was left a salty, muddy mess. "My parents are going to kill me," she said.

While we waited, she told us how they came to get stuck. They were all students at Lone Peak High School in Highland, Utah, about two and a half hours away. All of them were seniors except Kayla, who was a junior.

"We had the day off from school today, so instead of going to the amusement park with all the other kids, we decided to drive out here and do some filming. We are all [planning to be] film majors, and all of us will be going to the best film school at Utah Valley University. Graduation is next week."

Kayla and a couple of the other students told me about the movie they intended to make on the salt flats. They said it was a comedy, but when they explained the plot, I didn't think it sounded too funny—they'd sought out a desolate setting for a movie about a guy who had been living by himself after the apocalypse.

It was probably one of those dark comedies that I don't seem to understand.

Eventually their friends arrived with another tow rope, but together the two ropes were still not long enough to reach from the Escape's back bumper to their stranded Toyota out on the salt. Then a man driving a camper pulled up and said he had a tow rope as well, so combining all three allowed us to connect our Escape with Kayla's car.

"My parents are going to kill me," she said.

As I hooked up the three ropes and attached them to the rear of the Escape, Dave, who was driving it, gave a little tug. The rope quickly tightened, and I immediately fell down hard on that salty surface. I thought I broke my wrist, but luckily I was only bruised. I felt kind of stupid in front of all the students and assembled spectators.

I got up, dusted myself off, and told Dave to give it some more gas. Slowly, the car was pulled from the salty muck and into the parking lot. The teens were very appreciative, but still very dirty. I thought they should have started filming a movie the moment they got stuck in the salty yuck—now that would have been a comedy.

We all said goodbye and went our separate ways.

Nice kids, and it felt good to be Good Samaritans.

By stringing three tow ropes together, we were able to use our Escape to yank Kayla's car from its salty grave. They were good kids, all planning to attend film classes in college, and we were glad to help out.

Pacific **4** ▶ Standard Time

On this Highway 50 downhill, with a slight wind at our tail, we were able to achieve 63 miles per hour, by far the fastest speed on this journey. Henry Ford would be pleased that the original bearings his workmen installed almost one hundred years ago were still operating perfectly.

1. We were hungry, but Wendover is a strange place to find lunch. The place Michael had recommended, the Salt Flats Café, had changed hands and was now an Indian restaurant. We were not in the mood for that, so we drove into town.

Wendover is a border town split between two states: Utah and Nevada. There are lots of casinos on the "wild" Nevada side of town, but relatively few places to eat. Conversely, there are plenty of gas stations and fast-food places on the relatively conservative Utah side, but none where we cared to dine. (Remember what I said about McDonald's?) We saw one casino with a sign saying it had an Italian restaurant, but after we parked our cars and walked through what seemed to be miles of slot machines and roulette tables, we found out the restaurant was closed.

Fuel:
165.03 GALLONS
Distance:
2,942 MILES

Las Vegas it's not, but I suppose gamblers from Salt Lake City and the surrounding areas can come and let their hair down in a less conservative environment.

We decided to eat at the Shell station, of all places, while we were filling up with fuel. They had very good tacos.

After lunch, we drove a couple of blocks over to the historic Wendover Airfield. This was the airport from which the B-29 Superfortress bomber *Enola Gay* took off to fly to the Pacific, where it would drop the atom bomb over Hiroshima, Japan, in 1945. We were driving around the small airport looking for something interesting when a bright green shape caught our attention. It was a very cool-looking experimental aircraft that was taxiing around the airport's runways. It was very space age, in complete contrast to the Model T we were driving.

Cross that line, and enter not only another state but also another time zone. Wendover is a city split between two states and two cultures; one side has casinos and gambling, the other fast food restaurants and gas stations.

Michael went into the airport's administration building to see if we could gain access to the runway with our car in order to take photos of these two contrasting vehicles side by side. The airport manager was all for it. They weren't very busy that day, anyway, and I think he liked the idea a lot.

He told us to drive *Something* down to the far security gate, which he would open for us. Once we were on the tarmac, we had to locate the aircraft's owner, who had by now exited his plane and walked into the terminal. When he came back out,

Michael asked him if we could do a photo shoot with the two vehicles. He agreed.

He told us his name was Dieter Moenig, and he was a German now living in the state of Washington.

"My plane is called an AutoGyro," he said. "It's a kit that is made in Germany. It took me three hundred hours to build.

"I built another plane a long time ago, a Glasair, but that one took me 1,600 hours to build."

Dieter told us his AutoGyro is powered by a turbocharged four-cylinder Rotax gas engine that makes about 115 horsepower—enough to power the 680-pound craft as fast as 85 miles per hour, although he cruises at 70.

After our photos, Moenig started taxiing toward the runway. He intended to fly home by that evening. I don't know anything about flying, and not much about planes, but this machine looked well made; if he had invited me to take a ride with him, I would have jumped into the two-seater without hesitation.

Maybe that could be the subject of my next book: *AutoGyro Coast to Coast*!

I grew up on Long Island near a facility called Gyrodyne in Stony Brook, New York. The company manufactured gyroplanes—or, as they called them, gyrocopters—that were powered by lightweight, powerful, air-cooled Porsche

The longtime cowboy landmark that has stood in Wendover for more than fifty years. Once part of a sign in front of a hotel, the neon sign can be seen from miles away at night.

AUTOGYRO

Gyroplanes were first developed in 1923, but with the advent of helicopters and their popularity during World War II, the earlier rotorcraft were largely forgotten. In the 1980s, however, a resurgence of interest in non-fixed-wing aircraft began brewing, especially outside of the United States.

They work like this: as opposed to a helicopter, whose large, overhead blade is driven by an engine, the engine on a gyro drives a small vertical blade in the rear. The large rotor instead spins freely to provide lift, put in motion by the smaller blade. Because it is a forward propelled, or pusher, aircraft, a gyro cannot hover.

Engine failure in a gyro is not a concern, because the craft can softly land without power. Takeoff and landing can be accomplished in as little as 50 to 100 feet. A gyro costs about one-tenth as much as a helicopter and is as easy to maintain as a motorcycle.

AutoGyros like Dieter's are manufactured in Hildesheim, Germany, and marketed in the United States by AutoGyro USA, Stevensville, Maryland. Depending on the model, they can be powered by one of several Rotax gas-powered engines.

It certainly got my attention, and I started to think about how I was going to convince Pat that I needed one.

THE *ENOLA GAY* AND WENDOVER AIR FIELD

Before the United States dropped atomic bombs on Japan, which ultimately ended World War II, the Air Force needed to practice releasing the most potent armament in history. The man in charge of the program, Air Force Colonel Paul Tibbets, chose the Wendover (Utah) Air Field because of its distance from population centers and proximity to thousands of square miles of desert for pilots to train in isolation. A total of 155 "test" bombs were dropped in the desert in preparation for the Japanese assault.

New B-29s were ordered that featured lighter engines with fuel injection, reversible electric propellers, and pneumatic bomb doors. Each had a modified holding area to cradle the bomb. The *Enola Gay*, a B-29 similar to the *Lucky Lady* that Dave, Michael, and I had viewed at the Strategic Air Command Museum in Nebraska several days before, was assigned the task. The plane was named after Enola Gay Tibbets, the mother of its pilot, Colonel Tibbets.

At 2:45 a.m. on the morning of August 6, 1945, the *Enola Gay* departed from the Mariana Islands and became the first airplane to drop an atomic bomb, codenamed Little Boy, at 9:15 a.m. over the city of Hiroshima, Japan. Three days later, the B-20 *Bockscar* dropped another bomb, codenamed Fat Man, over the city of Nagasaki. The destruction was unprecedented, and the bombings quickly brought about Japan's surrender and an end to World War II.

By the end of 1946, all B-29s and their crews and equipment had been removed from Wendover, leaving what had been one of the most active air bases in the United States abandoned.

356 engines. They were mostly sold to the military, but I know that some got into private hands. I have always been curious about these flying machines, but hadn't seen one.

We stayed parked at the airport for a long time, wanting to see Dieter and his AutoGyro take off for the heavens. He taxied back and forth and back and forth for a very long time, probably getting his GPS adjusted for the long trip back to Washington. Finally, his bright green craft sped up and gently lifted off the ground. It was graceful and beautiful. Once he disappeared into the distance, so did we.

2. Entering Nevada was significant for a few reasons. One, it's in the Pacific Time Zone, so we got one more free hour—*ka-ching!*

Two, at 490 miles wide, it would be the largest state we'd cross. And three, after Nevada, only California would remain.

Driving southwest toward Ely, Nevada, it felt good to be back on the Lincoln Highway again, here known as US Route 93, and off the busy and high-speed I-80. For the past couple of days we had exclusively driven I-80, which was a limited-access, divided highway with 80-mile-per-hour speed limits. Being back on a slower two-lane was a relief for Dave and me, and I suppose it was for *Something* as well.

We drove at about the same speed as we had on I-80, 55 to 58 miles per hour. But unlike when we were on that busy interstate highway, on this long, lonely, arrow-straight road, we were virtually the only car.

The man at Wendover Airfield had recommended that we fill up with fuel before leaving Wendover, warning us there wasn't another gas station for 100 miles. Indeed, we drove miles and miles and miles on straight, empty roads, as far as the eye could see. But then . . .

"Dave, hold on, I see a curve coming up," I told him jokingly.

We both leaned into the corner in order to assist *Something* with the amazing g-force we were generating. Not.

"Whew, we made it through that one," I told Dave. "Let's hope there are not too many more of those. I'm not sure I can handle the physical and emotional stresses."

3. It had been a slow but steady climb ever since we left Wendover, ultimately reaching 6,500 feet. To use a running analogy again, it was like running up First Avenue in Manhattan, the 16-mile mark in the New York City Marathon. The incline is completely undetectable in a car, but on foot, it's an uphill slog all the way to the Bronx.

Something took this incline with ease, traveling at 55 miles per hour all the way. For having such a small engine, the car displayed an amazing amount of torque.

We were driving through open grazing land, meaning we crossed a couple of those steel cattle grates in the road that keep livestock on one side or the other. We saw some cows on occasion, but mostly just scrub brush and desert grasses all the way to the mountains in the far distance.

"Watch out, Dave," I said. "I think I see another curve coming up . . ."

4. When we first started driving *Something* at the beginning of this trip, she was pretty much an untested product—in retrospect, probably not the wisest choice to take on a long-distance trip. Owner Nathan had driven her

OPPOSITE: The airfield in Wendover was a top-secret facility during World War II. It was where pilots practiced dropping dummy atomic bombs, and where the *Enola Gay* actually departed from when it dropped the bomb on Hiroshima, Japan.

ABOVE: Today folks rent the old hangers at Wendover to store and repair their vintage aircraft.

FOLLOWING PAGES: The Wendover Air Field is no longer top secret; it's a recreational airport. We noticed this AutoGyro and talked the owner, Dieter Moenig, into allowing us to park *Something* next to his plane. Talk about a contrast in transportation!

around locally in northern Virginia, trouble free, but on this 3,400-plus mile trip, our fingers were crossed.

When we left the congestion of New York, New Jersey, and Philadelphia, we kept to a steady 52 to 53 miles per hour. This was due to us not knowing the car's comfortable cruising speed—we didn't want to break the engine. Because we had a long way to go, we didn't want to overtax the mechanical bits.

But as we became more comfortable with the car (and I suppose it became more comfortable with us), we slowly increased the speed to 54, maybe even 55 miles per hour. Early in the trip, if we saw a speed of 57 mph on our GPS speedometer function, that point had been uncharted territory—where no T had gone before. We were afraid that a huge mechanical malfunction might occur if we subjected the engine to too many RPMs.

Just in case that happened, Dave was prepared. At home, he had a spare Model T engine and gearbox already loaded on a trailer, along with an engine hoist and all the tools necessary to swap motors. His plan was that he could get a friend to drive that engine out to meet us and we could be back on the road in a matter of just a few days.

Fuel:
172.37 GALLONS
Distance:
3,060 MILES
· · · · · · · · · ·

Now that we'd hit Nevada, with only one state to go, we were pressing the car a little bit harder—especially on Highway 93, which was straight and smooth. Dave got *Something* up to 58, even 59 miles per hour. We were helped by a tail wind for the first time, having been battling head winds for much of the trip.

Just as I was thinking that maybe we could hit 60 miles per hour before we reached the Golden Gate Bridge, Dave hit 62, then 63!

"I think under the right conditions, with a slight downhill and the wind at our tail, we could hit 70," he said. "But I don't want to blow it up with such a short way to still go."

5. When we pulled into the town of Ely, Nevada (pronounced EE-lee), the first thing I noticed were all the old cars. Almost immediately we passed four fenced yards within a couple of miles of each other, each housing a selection of old cars and trucks. Among them were lots of 1940s and 1950s Fords and Chevys, even a Model T coupe parked near the road.

When we drove by that T, *Something* was instantly smitten.

The next thing we noticed were lots of high-performance cars with numbers on their doors. It was obvious that there was some kind of rally in town.

The receptionist at Hotel Nevada, our lodging for the evening, explained that the Silver State Classic Challenge—a high-speed, open-road racing event— was passing through Ely that night.

"They close off roads to the public and let these cars run flat out," she said. "It's the only rally like it in the United States."

I had heard of the Silver State Classic before but never paid much attention to it, probably because I live on the East Coast and it's so far away. I noticed men and women walking around the hotel's casino lobby wearing automotive-related shirts, jackets and hats. At a racer's party across the street from Hotel Nevada, I asked one man what kind of car he was driving in the rally, and he told me, a Mercedes-Benz AMG C-55.

Passing sites like this got my attention: a field of old cars and trucks sitting in the desert. Because of the dry climate and almost zero rainfall, the sheet metal on these cars might still be usable, unless they are full of bullet holes.

SILVER STATE CLASSIC CHALLENGE

Driving at high speeds on public roads, legally, sounds almost too good to be true, but Silver State Classic entrants do that each May. Considered the fastest open road race in the world, its participants race high-performance cars 90 miles across the Nevada desert on a temporarily closed section of Highway 318.

While most cars competing are Mustangs and Corvettes, Ferraris, Lamborghinis, and even Mercedes station wagons are regularly entered. In May of 2012, the ultimate event record speed of 217.557 miles per hour was set by Jim Peruto in a NASCAR-modified Dodge Charger.

The event is run with the cooperation of the Nevada State Department of Transportation and the White Pine Chamber of Commerce. The rules for car preparation and the safety equipment required are extensive. Because there are no safety barriers, spectating is not permitted. The only way to see the race is by volunteering to be one of the course workers who keep other cars off the highway.

Sponsors include the Showboat Hotel and Casino and Sam's Town Hotel and Gambling Hall.

Celebrities occasionally participate in the Classic, including Jon Schneider of *Dukes of Hazzard* fame, who has competed several times in the *General Lee*.

"I'm an open-road-racing enthusiast," said Blue Offutt, a man from Surprise, Arizona. "I've done about fifty of these rallies so far, in Nevada, Texas, and Nebraska. I haven't tried one in Mexico yet."

The enthusiasm for these high-speed events runs in his family.

"My wife, Deanna, is my current navigator, but my mother-in-law, Kathy, Deanna's mom, was my original navigator."

His mother-in-law. I hadn't heard that one before.

Offutt had just started racing the Mercedes recently.

"Before that we raced a 1993 twin-turbo Mazda that put out 300 horsepower to the wheels."

He said he has driven his Mazda to 171 miles per hour. His Mercedes has already reached 175. I asked him whether accidents occur during these rallies.

"Ninety-nine percent of accidents on these events happen because of tire failure," he said.

Offutt treats his Mercedes like a true race car. "We don't normally drive these cars on the street," he said. "I trailer my car to these events."

I wandered around the couple of hundred other racers until I met a pair of mature-looking guys who were sitting at a table, eating hors d'oeuvres. I introduced myself to Jim Ricke and Jean Lowery, both from Lebanon, Oregon, who said they volunteer annually as gatekeepers for the Silver State Classic.

OPPOSITE: The apparently famous Hotel Nevada in Ely, Nevada. When we arrived, we saw a number of high-performance cars in town with numbers on them. It turned out they were using Hotel Nevada as headquarters for the Silver State Classic, a high-speed race across the desert on lonely roads.

"Gatekeepers keep other vehicles from entering the closed road where cars are racing," said Lowery. "We have to be out there at 5:00 a.m. in the morning and until about 4:00 p.m. in the afternoon. It's a long day.

"Cars at the start are waved off at one-minute intervals."

Lowery explained that they are in charge of gate 92, 52 miles into the 90-mile course.

"If a car is going 15 miles per hour slower than their target speed, they are disqualified," he said.

Neither gentlemen had ever ridden in one of these race cars, but both would jump at the opportunity.

"My first car was a 1937 Ford coupe with mechanical brakes," said Jean, perhaps feeling he had to give me his automotive qualifications. "These days I like to ride around rural Nevada on the back roads. Once when I was passing through Ely, this race was going on, so I signed up as a gatekeeper."

Jim had a similar initiation.

"This filled my bucket list," he said. "I discovered it once when I was riding my Harley-Davidson from Reno to Tampa, Florida."

Both Jim and Jean told me that event organizers do not reimburse volunteers for travel or lodging expenses.

HOTEL NEVADA

The hundred-room Hotel Nevada was built for a cost of $100,000 in 1929—around $1.5 million in today's dollars. Until 1935, the six-story building was the tallest in the city of Ely. Many celebrities and politicians have lodged in the hotel since then, and many of their names are emblazoned in sidewalk marquees along Aultman Street, the town's main road and part of the Lincoln Highway. Some of those celebrities include Ingrid Bergman, Jackie Cooper, Mickey Rooney, Senator Harry Reid, President Lyndon B. Johnson, First Lady Pat Nixon, and stuntman Evel Knievel.

Several movies have also been filmed at Hotel Nevada, including *Operation Haylift* (1950), *My Blueberry Nights* (2008), and *Play Dead* (2009).

Between 1920 and 1933, when alcohol consumption became illegal during the era of Prohibition, Hotel Nevada continued to offer its guests opportunities to imbibe moonshine and "bathtub gin." Similarly, when gambling was made illegal between 1910 and 1931—and the casino converted into a bank and a drug store—the hotel secretly offered its customers opportunities to continue gambling.

After a number of ownership changes, the hotel was temporarily closed during the economic downturn in the mid-1980s. Various ownership partnerships operated the hotel for the next three decades until 2014, when it was purchased by John Gaughan, a third-generation casino owner. Gaughan said the casino and hotel reminded him of El Cortez, the venue his grandfather once owned in Las Vegas. He added new carpeting, updated the casino's gambling machines, and added live sportsbook gambling. He also refurbished the restaurant, which was rebranded as Denny's when it reopened in 2017.

"We're here because we love the people," said Jim.

I asked Jean just how fast the cars go on the 90-mile course.

"The record for the 90-mile course is just twenty minutes, which averaged 217 miles per hour," he said. "When that Dodge Charger crossed the finish line, it was going 254 miles per hour.

"But it was not like any Dodge Charger you've ever seen."

6. Staying at Hotel Nevada was rustic, to say the least.

It's an old hotel that has seen lots of use over the past ninety years. The lobby features a casino, and Denny's is the featured onsite restaurant. And smoking is allowed everywhere.

Living in North Carolina, where thankfully smoking is banned in all public indoor spaces, I've become so spoiled. When I smell tobacco smoke, it instantly gets my attention. Yucko.

I remember waking up as a child to my father's Lucky Strike cigarettes, and in later years walking into a pub and enduring a cloud of smoke just to have a beer. Oh, and going to a rock concert was not complete without coming home with stinky clothes, probably a mixture of both tobacco and nontobacco smoke. Even when I was in business years later, I remember flying on commercial airliners that were simply secondhand smoking chambers.

All these memories came rushing back to me when I checked into Hotel Nevada. But it was an authentic historic hotel smack dab in the middle of the Lincoln Highway, which is why we chose it. That, plus the room rates were really low.

So in service to you, the reader, we took one for the team and shacked up there for the night.

The mattress in my room had obviously seen lots of action over the years, that's for sure. As had the pillows. I wouldn't take off my socks, but instead used them as slippers. And I prayed that my mouth wouldn't fall open in the night, allowing my tongue to touch the bedspread.

But, as it turned out, I wouldn't sleep much anyway. There was "activity" in the room next door or above us, which made sleep a challenge. The lyrics to Paul Simon's "Duncan" came to mind at about 1:45 a.m.

Enough said about that. I think I will check TripAdvisor the next time I need a hotel room in Ely.

One of the racers, Blue Offutt, races his street-legal Mercedes AMG at speeds up to 175 miles per hour! His wife is the co-driver/navigator, but his mother-in-law used to be his navigator!

7. This was not the first time I had been in Ely. On my second drive across the United States in 2001, when Peter Egan and I took the Cobra from Walnut Creek, near Oakland, California, to North Carolina, we stopped there to have a noisy exhaust manifold repaired. The gasket between the manifold and the downpipe had blown out, and I just couldn't stand hearing that rumble for 2,000 more miles. So we went to a repair shop in town and had it repaired—$15. Cheap.

The mechanics got a kick over repairing an authentic Cobra in their little shop. While I was there, I had them add on two chrome exhaust tips to snazz up the rear. At least it would resemble the Cobra model kit I once had as a kid.

Soon we were on our way with a quiet and better-looking exhaust.

8. In the morning, Michael and I downed a hearty Denny's breakfast and walked out onto the sidewalk in front of the hotel. Dave had not only serviced *Something* by then but already had it warmed up and ready to go.

The temperature on my iPhone said 28 degrees, but in the full sunshine, it was spectacular. There was no wind, and we felt the promise of a beautiful day ahead.

We headed west out of Ely on Highway 50, which is nicknamed the Loneliest Road in America. Whether it is or not, it is a beautiful and desolate drive on smooth, scenic roads with some twists and some elevation changes. Interestingly, Dave's home in West Virginia is just a few miles from the eastern portion of Highway 50.

Our GPS altimeter told us we were at 7,500 feet above sea level when we arrived at the Little Antelope Summit, about halfway between Ely and Austin, Nevada. In the distance to the right was a spectacular view of Diamond Peak, a 10,614-foot beauty that was brilliant this morning. I felt we were driving through one of those more-beautiful-than-possible movie sets for a John Wayne western.

This is an ideal part of the country to do some serious driving. I could tell why those Silver State Classic participants love coming back to this region year after year.

After departing Ely, we passed through the first of the three towns, Eureka, about 80 miles into the drive. The town was a true step back in time; as we entered, we passed an old general store on the left that would likely have an interesting story or two to tell if it could talk.

West of Ely, Nevada, we took the historic Highway 50, known as the Loneliest Road in America. Lonely, yes, but also beautiful, and a road where *Something* was able to let her hair down . . .

HIGHWAY 50: THE LONELIEST
ROAD IN AMERICA

A July 1986 *Life* magazine story turned a barren section of Nevada roadway into a nationally celebrated piece of asphalt. Calling it "The Loneliest Road in America," the story warned motorists not to consider driving on the roadway unless they were confident of their survival skills. Nevada officials were quick to rebrand the rural two-lane, giving it a bad-boy reputation.

The stretch from Ely to the California border is 287 miles and passes through only three small towns. In his book *Blue Highways*, author William Least Heat-Moon said, "For the unhurried, this little-known highway is the best national road across the middle of the United States."

Highway 50 crosses several large desert valleys separated by numerous mountain ranges towering over the valley floors, in what is known as the Basin and Range province of the Great Basin. It has a diverse route through the state, traversing the resort communities of Lake Tahoe, the state capital in Carson City, historical sites such as Fort Churchill State Historic Park, petroglyphs, alpine forests, desert valleys, ghost towns, and Great Basin National Park.

The route was constructed over a historic corridor that was first used for the Pony Express and Central Overland Route and later for the Lincoln Highway. Before the formation of the US Highway System, most of US 50 in Nevada was designated State Route 2. The routing east of Ely has changed significantly from the original plans, the result of a rivalry between Nevada and Utah over which transcontinental route was better to serve California-bound traffic, the Lincoln Highway or the Victory Highway.

On Highway 50, the Lincoln Highway in central Nevada, the scene looks the same, north, south, east, or west. Except for pavement, the view along our route was identical. *Lincoln Highway Digital Image Collection, University of Michigan Library (Special Collections Library)*

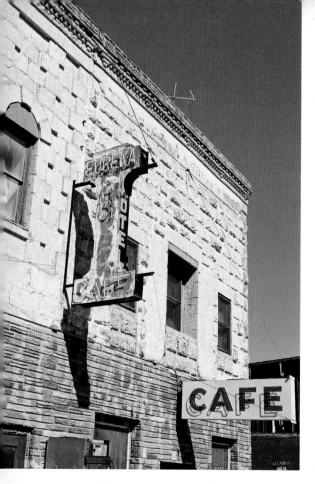

Eureka (population four hundred) is an old mining town, named after the call that miners made when they discovered a vein of either lead or silver. Because of heavy black smoke that once spewed from tall smokestacks at lead smelting plants, it was called the Pittsburgh of the West. At least fifty mines were dug in the town, producing gold and zinc in addition to the aforementioned lead and silver.

These days, Eureka is a sleepy town. It is estimated that 2,100 cars travel on Highway 50 per day on average, so the retail opportunities for potential shop owners are slim. A small marker still exists that identifies 22 miles of pavement as the General Motors Section, a section of road that General Motors Corporation funded for the amount of $100,000 in 1919.

One Eureka curiosity is the mostly collapsed remains of brick-lined underground tunnels that were built to ensure beer deliveries could be made from breweries to saloons during winter snows. As a secondary benefit to a larger swath of society, the tunnels could also be used to commute to school, although there was no word what would happen to the children once they reached the saloon.

Just outside of Eureka, Highway 50 seemed to go off into infinity. To our left and right were roads running perpendicular, seemingly to their own infinities. Some were paved, but most were dirt. It made me wish we had the time to explore a couple of these roads to see where they led—perhaps an old mining operation or a ghost town? Maybe a pot of gold? Sometimes I just like to see things off the beaten path, things that take some effort to get to.

In some ways, I'm still that adventurous fourteen-year-old kid looking for pirate's treasure. Or old cars.

9. The beauty of Highway 50 is beyond description. It's as if we were driving into a stunning coffee-table book.

The brilliant, cloudless blue sky and the snow-capped mountains in the distance gently spilling down to a green valley made for a spectacular backdrop as we headed west at a blazing 59 miles per hour. We've all seen these amazing images in print and on TV, but it is awe inspiring to experience this grandeur in person. I can't imagine what the earliest settlers heading west must have thought—or the first motorists on the Lincoln Highway.

As we climbed up a steep, 7,000-plus-foot grade, we were actually faster than another vehicle for once! A tanker truck hauling two trailers was crawling up the grade ahead of us.

"Think we can catch him?" Dave asked.

"Sure, we'll kick his ass," I said. I gripped the steering wheel tighter and pressed the accelerator. We eventually caught him as the elevation topped out at 7,200 feet. We were actually on his rear bumper, which is something we hadn't been able to do yet on this trip. When we reached the summit, the truck pulled aside and let us pass.

Dave and I high-fived each other and we gave a little blast of the *ahooooga* horn, which was now working again (we had purchased a new fuse the day before), as we blew the doors off that truck. At least figuratively speaking.

10. The tiny town of Austin, 70 miles from Eureka, was like an oasis in the desert, which I suppose it is. It took us about ninety minutes to commute from Eureka to Austin, but in a 1915 Lincoln Highway guide, motorists were warned of a five-hour drive that featured "some hard road, some gravel, a number of washes, some rough spots and some mountain grades." I'm glad that, 103 years later, those issues have been ironed out.

The 1915 Lincoln Highway Guide lists Austin's main-street speed limit at 6 miles per hour. It seems even *Something* could garner a speeding ticket in Austin with a limit like that!

Austin (population 250) was named after the Texas town of the same name and is among the oldest of the state's silver-mining towns. Rumor has it that the place quickly grew from zero to ten thousand residents when a Pony Express driver kicked a stone and discovered it was silver. The mines yielded silver ore for about ten years before workers moved on to mines in other areas. Most of the small towns surrounding Austin have become ghost towns.

We needed gas and food, and I was not the only one who needed a potty break.

We struck up a conversation with a couple of motorcyclists at a little diner in Austin whose BMW 1200 GSs were parked at the curb. I had seen these guys earlier in the day as they respectfully passed us.

They told us they had left their homes in Sacramento, California, twenty-eight days earlier and had travelled along the US–Mexican border, past the Gulf of Mexico, and into Florida. Compared with our primitive transport, these guys bragged about their heated hand grips and heated jackets! They were just as interested about our experiences as we were theirs.

Two other diners traveling eastbound heard us talking and struck up a conversation about our car. One thing led to another, and soon we were talking about old Corvettes and sports-car racing.

Then the name Briggs Cunningham came up, which I didn't expect to happen on the Loneliest Road in America in Austin, Nevada, that day. Well, I am a big fan and historian of Briggs Cunningham and his cars, so we enjoyed a few minutes talking about the powerful white cars with blue stripes. Eventually we said goodbye, and they went their way and we went ours.

Fuel:
181.33 GALLONS
Distance:
3,211 MILES
....

The town of Austin, Nevada, was only slightly more populated than Eureka. This former garage might also have once been a car dealership, but we couldn't find anyone who could tell us for sure.

Austin was about 150 miles west of Ely, or about halfway to that evening's destination of Reno. We filled up with food and continued on our beautiful ride through the desert.

Jim Lilliefors wrote in his 1993 book, *Highway 50: Ain't that America!*:

Until it reaches Fallon, Highway 50 cuts through what Nevada natives call Real Nevada. In Real Nevada, the range is still open, the air is pure and the cattle graze right out on the highway. During windstorms, the sky can become so choked with dust that the only thing a traveler can do is park his car on the highway and wait until it stops.

11. The road west of Austin was smooth, but the 1915 guide said to beware of washouts and cut-up roads as a result of double-teaming ore wagons. The 1918 guide goes further: "the ruts are so deep that we had to drive a little to the right or left of them in order not to scrape the poor car's abdomen entirely off. Between the ruts was a continuous deep line about 2 inches wide that I discovered was a trail of the crank case nut of many cars."

I don't think Nathan would have appreciated that.

It was a 100-mile-long drive from Austin to Fallon, the third town on Highway 50 between Ely and Reno.

I had thought we'd have some sort of mechanical malfunction by this point—after all, this car was ninety-two years old, and we were pushing it to its limits and beyond. So, in the event of that inevitable breakdown, Michael was prepared to document it as Dave and I feverishly worked on the side of the road to repair the problem.

The only problem was, it never happened, at least not yet.

But I still wanted that photo. So in the middle of nowhere on Highway 50 in Nevada, at a distant crossroad, I asked Dave to pull onto the dirt side road so we could simulate a repair.

Fuel:
187.75 GALLONS
Distance:
3,326 MILES
....

"What?" he said.

"Dave, I just want to have Michael take a photo as if we were broken down in the desert," I said.

So I talked him into jacking up the car and removing the rear wheel. This we did. Then, as Michael was shooting photos, I took that tire and rolled it down the road, as if I was walking toward infinity looking for a repair shop.

I just wanted you to know that photo was staged.

There, I feel better now.

12. Day 13 was an amazing day because we were just a few miles from the California state line. By lunchtime, we'd be entering our thirteenth and final state.

But first we had to grab breakfast. So we came down the elevator from the nineteenth floor of the Circus Circus hotel and casino, where we had spent the night, down to the street level and discovered . . . a car show!

Walking onto Virginia Street, there were hundreds of antiques, hot rods, and muscle cars. Since we had no place to be any time soon, we spent a couple of hours walking around the Spring Fever Revival, a free cruise-in that serves as a prelude to Hot Summer Nights in August. It's an annual event that has been running since 1986. We saw cool old cars and spoke with many people.

Dave brought *Something* down from the garage and parked it on the street next to another speedster made from a car called a Star, which I had never heard of before. This one had a Dodge engine and a Model A rear axle and was painted up like a fire chief's car. It and *Something* looked good parked side by side on the street.

We departed from the show before lunch and took I-80 out of Reno and toward the state line—but not before stopping for a photo op on the eastbound side at a scenic pull-off.

I noticed in Brian Butko's *Greetings from the Lincoln Highway* that there was a set of historic bridge rails displayed in a rest area on a eastbound stretch of I-80. I figured it might be worth a photo op, so we drove west one exit past

Shhhh, don't tell anybody, but this photo is a fake. Because *Something* was running so well and never broke down we staged this flat-tire scene on a side road directly off Highway 50.

the rest area, took an exit, and doubled back to see these landmarks, which were constructed sometime around 1914. In 1970, for safekeeping, they were removed from the bridge by some forward-thinking locals and the Department of Transportation and put on display in the rest area.

While we were there, I wanted to grab my notebook out of the Escape, which was locked, so I asked Michael for his keys. I grabbed the notebook and scribbled some notes about the bridge rails. Then Dave and I jumped right back into the car and drove off.

We had done this a number of times at photo locations. Michael usually had additional photos to take, but he could quickly catch up with us. So Dave and I scooted westbound along I-80, toward the California state line, just 5 miles away. There it was: the "Welcome to California" sign.

We pulled over to the shoulder and waited for Michael so he could take a photo of *Something* at the verge of entering our last state. And waited.

We spent the night at the Circus-Circus casino/resort in Reno because the rooms were cheap and readily available. When we woke up, there was a car show going on! Dave parked *Something* next to a red speedster.

"Michael must have found something else to photograph," I said to Dave.

After ten minutes, I called Michael's cell phone, only to get his voicemail.

"Michael, are you OK?" I said in a message. "We're waiting for you at the 'Welcome to California' sign."

Another five minutes and I called him again. Still the recording.

Five minutes later, I called it again.

I sent a text: "Are you OK?"

I was worried. Dave and I decided to go to the next exit, turn around, and go back to where we had last seen him thirty minutes earlier. Now I was really worried, and the worst was going through my head.

I called Michael's cell phone two or three more times.

What was I going to tell his wife? We couldn't get back to the scenic pull-out soon enough.

Dave steered *Something* to the right, and I saw the silver Escape parked where it was.

At least he didn't have an accident, I thought. But maybe he'd had a heart attack . . .

As we drove closer, however, there was Michael standing next to the Escape, smiling, with his

camera in his hand. Suddenly it came to me why he never followed us or returned my cell phone calls.

I'd never returned his car keys; they were still in my pocket. He walked up to *Something*, smiling and shaking his head.

"You have no idea how happy I am to see you," I said. "I'm so sorry."

He had been standing in the bright sunshine without shade or a hat.

"No problem," he said. "I thought I'd just call you about the keys, but my phone was locked in the Escape."

Dave knew how relieved I was. Michael has been my photography partner for years, so he is like a brother to me. Glad you're OK, man.

This is the fifth book that Michael and I have collaborated on. We have it down to a science: I interview the subjects and he shoots the photos, and he's always listening to make sure he's shooting what I am talking about.

I hope I don't have to work with another photographer for the rest of my writing career.

. . . .

13. OK. Welcome to California, take two.
Dave and I drove the 5 miles back to the sign, this time with Michael behind us in the Escape. Once we got there, he jumped out and had started to shoot photos of *Something* in front of the sign when a California State Trooper pulled over with his lights flashing.

Darn. I realized it was probably illegal to pull over on an interstate highway for photos. We'd probably get a ticket.

The trooper walked right up to Dave in the driver's seat and said, "You're busted!"

He was as serious as a heart attack.

Damn, what does that mean? I thought. *Will we go to jail for this?*

ABOVE: I mistakenly put the keys to Michael's Escape in my pocket, and when Dave and I drove off in *Something*, we stranded Michael in the rest area without access to his cell phone, which was locked in the car. When he never showed up, I imagined the worst had happened.

FOLLOWING PAGES: When we finally saved Michael, he followed us to this California sign for a photo of *Something* entering our thirteenth and final state. While he was shooting, though, a California Highway Patrol officer pulled up and had a good laugh having us believe we were breaking the law.

We stopped for lunch in Truckee, California, at Moody's Bistro in the Historic Truckee Hotel.

Then the trooper broke into a huge smile.

"I saw the sign on the back of your car, 'California or Bust.' Well, you made it to California—now you're busted."

He roared in laughter.

I was so relieved. He kindly held up the heavy I-80 traffic and allowed us to merge back onto the highway.

What an emotional roller coaster we'd experienced over the past hour. I hoped we could just motor along without drama for a little while.

14. We pulled into the town of Truckee, about 20 miles into California. It was close to lunchtime, and Michael said he knew of a cool restaurant that he and his wife, Danielle, have visited.

Sounded good to me.

We followed his silver Escape to a hip-looking place on Main Street, the historic Truckee Hotel. Inside the hotel was our destination, Moody's Bistro. We bellied up to the bar and ordered sandwiches and cold water.

It had turned out to be a nice day after all, despite the morning's near–heart stoppers. The weather was cool, breezy, sunny.

After lunch and an ice cream cone we headed over to Donner Lake for a photo shoot near the historic Donner Pass. Michael had used this location for previous photo sessions for car companies like BMW and magazines like the Porsche Club of America's *Panorama*, and he suggested that it might be a perfect backdrop for *Something*. We kept climbing and climbing, passing two girls jogging on the side of the road.

When we finally reached the lake, which is still officially on the Lincoln Highway, it was amazing. There was a fair amount of snow on the surrounding mountains; afterward we found out that there had been a snowstorm in the upper elevations just a day or two earlier. I could tell why people come there as a vacation destination or retirement living, since you wouldn't wind up in Donner by accident.

As we finished shooting, those two young ladies whom we'd seen running at the bottom of the mountain came jogging by us, talking and laughing. I am a lifelong runner, but I avoid elevation like the plague. These girls were impressive athletes.

As they passed, I asked how long they had been running.

"Oh, a few miles," they said. "Since the bottom."

15. One of the people who had been following our Facebook posts was Matt Ryan, who lives in Sacramento. In a message, he said he also owned a Model T speedster like ours, as well as a vacation cabin near the Donner Pass.

Fuel:
196.13 GALLONS
Distance:
3,448 MILES

"You guys are invited to spend the night in the cabin and my girlfriend can make a nice home-cooked dinner for you," he posted.

Let's see: free room and board, a home-cooked meal, and a car enthusiast to boot? That worked for us. And how I yearned for some home-cooked food.

"In the morning you can follow my speedster from the cabin and I'll show you the best roads down to Sacramento," he said.

What could be wrong with this scenario?

So after the Donner Lake photo shoot, we headed in Matt's direction.

DONNER PASS

Early settlers traveling to California were challenged with where to cross the Sierra Nevada mountain range. A common route was a low notch several miles west of Truckee, California, which required a steep climb from the east, but offered a gentle downward grade to the west.

In November 1846, a westbound party of eighty-one travelers led by George Donner was halted by a heavy early snowfall at the pass and they were unable to continue. The party was forced to spend the winter on the steep east side of the range. The winter was brutal, and many reached the point of starvation. In the spring, only forty-five lived to reach their California destination. Some of the survivors had resorted to cannibalism, which gave the pass its morbid reputation. After the tragedy, the pass was named after the Donner Party.

In an episode of déjà vu just more than a century later, although not nearly as tragic, a train with 222 passengers and crew became stranded in heavy snow just seven miles west of the Donner Pass in January 1952. Unable to move in either direction, the passengers were forced to live aboard the snowbound train for three days. When a road was finally plowed to allow emergency vehicles, the passengers and crew were rescued and brought to a nearby lodge to recover.

Today the Donner Pass is home to a thriving recreational and skiing resort community, but winters are still brutal. Annual snow regularly accumulates to more than 400 inches, making it one of America's snowiest regions. At least six times since 1880, annual accumulated snow has reached from 775 to more than 800 inches.

16.

"A friend has been following your progress on Facebook, and messaged me that these guys are driving a speedster from New York, to San Francisco and they're looking for cool places to stay," Matt said. "That's how I found out about you."

He gave me directions to his rural cabin.

"Make a hard right at the road sign and go down the long dirt road," he said. "Keep going past all the cabins until you see one with a Model T speedster in front of it. That's mine."

Matt and his girlfriend, Maya Beneli, live in Sacramento, but they spend most weekends one hour away at their mountain cabin in Emigrant Gap, west of the Donner Pass. If it was our desire to live like early motorists whenever possible on this trip, this is exactly what we had in mind. When we pulled down the driveway, it was like we had stepped ninety years back in time. When they heard our car chugging down the driveway, Matt and Maya stepped outside their cabin to meet us.

Their primitive cabin, built from a kit in 1937, was in need of repair when Matt bought five years ago.

"It was mostly not insulated," he said. "The walls are made of tongue-and-groove boards that slid together."

Something, meet *California*. Matt Ryan had been tracking our progress across the country and sent us a message. "Would you guys be interested in staying in our cabin overnight?" We gladly accepted and were surprised to discover that Matt also had a Rajo-powered Model T speedster called the *California Special*.

Interestingly, the cabin had been used as a full-time home for a period, despite no insulation and despite being located deep in a forest that regularly receives huge wintertime snow.

"Last winter we had so much snow that we rode sleds off the roof," he said.

During our May visit, some of that snow was still on the ground, so in keeping with our desire to keep this trip truly vintage, we buried a six-pack of locally brewed beer in a bank of snow to keep it cold. The beer, appropriately enough, was named Sumpin' Special.

17. Matt restored his speedster a number of years ago as a senior project while he was still in high school.

"It's a 1915 Model T that was built into a speedster a long time ago," he said.

"I found it on Brandon Island in the Sacramento Delta. Most of the islands in the delta are lower than the surrounding water, so there is a levee system. This car was underwater in a barn for at least ten months."

Matt told me the car was not complete when he acquired it, but it had a brass emblem on the radiator shell that read "California Special." He showed me the project summary he produced before graduation. It was quite impressive to see what a serious restorer he was as a teenager.

Matt (right) and his girlfriend, Maya Beneli, spend most weekends at their mountain cabin near Donner Pass. They said it provides a nice contrast to their Sacramento, California, homes.

Fifteen years later, he was still a serious car guy. Besides the speedster, he also owned a 1926 Model T sedan, a 1966 Mustang, a really cool 1959 Rambler Super Cross Country wagon, and a first-generation Bronco. Matt also hosts an annual driving tour for vintage cars, which is called Ryan's Rambles.

Dave and I felt proud of our accomplishment of driving *Something* from New York to California, but our feat paled in comparison to what Matt had accomplished with his T. He once drove the speedster to Alaska's Arctic Circle, camping out every night in the small trailer he towed behind his car! This guy was a serious adventurer.

A couple of Matt's friends stopped over to see our car and learn about our trip. Aaron Johnson and his son, Adler, drove their 1929 Model A woody wagon, and Aaron's father-in-law, Bill, drove his really sweet 1965 Volkswagen Beetle. Maya made us an amazing meal that couldn't be beat, and we sat around talking cars and Model Ts until late into the night.

18. Dave, Michael, and I slept in the cabin while Maya and Matt stayed in an adjacent motorhome he keeps on the property.

None of us was in a particular hurry to get up and out of bed the following morning. I was snuggled down in my bed, not too eager to begin the day—or for this adventure to end.

According to my GPS, we were 170 miles from Lincoln Park at the Golden Gate Bridge. It had been an amazing couple of weeks, and I just wanted it to stretch out a little bit longer. But we eventually forced ourselves up, drawn to the kitchen by the smell of Maya's wonderful cooking. Her pancakes were spot on.

Our plan was to follow Matt and Maya in their speedster down to Sacramento, then continue to San Francisco. As we drove down Matt's long dirt driveway toward the paved road, Dave made an interesting observation.

"This long driveway probably resembles what the original Lincoln Highway looked like through California a hundred years ago," he said. "But thankfully we're not going through axle-deep mud."

Amen.

The next morning we followed Matt and Maya in their speedster as they showed us some of the prettiest, most dynamic roads of our trip thus far. Dave and Matt had a blast driving these Model Ts on the rural roads en route to Sacramento.

19. Matt and Maya offered to show us some of the more interesting back roads from the mountain cabin to Sacramento.

"Just follow my speedster and we'll have a good time," Matt said.

Our speedster caravan must have been quite a treat for enthusiasts out on this early Sunday morning. Vintage MGs and Porsches, whose owners were enjoying the roads like we were, all gave us a thumbs-up. And because both our

SCOTT PRUETT

Scott Pruett is a American racing driver who has competed in virtually every form of motorsport. Starting as an eight-year-old in go karts, he won ten professional karting championships before moving to sports cars.

In road racing, Pruett won three Trans Am and two IMSA GTO championships. Switching to Indycars in the 1990s, he earned two wins, fifteen top-three finishes, and five pole starting positions. He moved to NASCAR in 2000, achieving only one top-ten finish before returning to road racing with the Ganassi Racing team. During his twelve years with the team, he earned five Grand Am championships. Pruett has won the 24 Hours of Daytona five times, won the 12 Hours of Sebring once overall and once in-class, and won his class at the 24 Hours of Le Mans.

He was inducted into the Motorsports Hall of Fame in 2017.

Michael's friend, road racing champion Scott Pruett, met us near his home in Auburn, California.

Pruett and his wife, Judy, own Pruett Vineyards in Auburn, California, where they produce award-winning wines. The couple has also written a series of auto-racing-themed children's books.

cars had similarly modified engines with Rajo cylinder heads, we were able to drive those back roads in a true spirited manner.

They were nothing short of amazing, many of them authentic Lincoln Highway routes. The two speedsters scooted through those roads like the sports cars they were.

For me, this was the most fun driving of the trip so far, and judging from the grin on Dave's face, he was having a blast as well.

We stopped only once, to photograph the two cars next to a Lincoln Highway marker. I'd say that Michael had quite a chore keeping up with us in the Escape that morning.

We ended in Auburn for a piece of pie at Ikeda's Pie Shop, apparently a local landmark. All the pies looked amazing, but I had to pick just one, so I went with blueberry. And it was so good.

Michael surprised us by having a special guest waiting for us at Ikeda's. Because he has been an auto racing photographer for so many years, Michael is

We met a couple of enthusiasts who were replacing the fuel pump on their vintage Dodge touring car. One of them had heard of our cross-country trip, which I thought was totally amazing.

friends with a number of people in the racing world, and when we pulled into the parking lot, champion sports-car driver Scott Pruett was waiting for us. He lives in Auburn and owns a vineyard there.

And he's a car guy who loves to build hot rods in addition to racing sports cars.

I first met Scott when I was public relations director at Charlotte Motor Speedway in the 1980s. He had recently been crowned the King of Karting by the World Karting Association and was just becoming involved in professional sports-car racing.

But on this morning, he enjoyed seeing and learning about our two speedsters.

After we had all enjoyed a piece of pie, the three of us said goodbye to Scott, who went back to his vineyard, and to Matt and Maya, who continued on to Sacramento. We continued south on the Lincoln Highway for a few miles, then turned left onto Highway 49, eastbound. We were taking a side trip to meet a metal shaper in Camino, whom Dave had been communicating with for a few months.

En route to Camino, we passed through a town by the name of Cool, California. A mile later, we passed the Cool Elementary School. Who wouldn't want to get their education there?

Highway 49 was one of those dream roads you only see on TV commercials. There were huge elevation changes with sweeping switchbacks, and the scenery was loaded with lush foliage, tall trees, and horse farms. The inner Porsche racing driver in Dave became apparent—*Something* was tooling through these roads like a 911 Carrera. These roads were the most dynamic we had experienced yet on this trip.

It was here that *Something*'s amazing road-holding characteristics became evident. Dave had the car drifting through turns more like a sports car than a 1920s grocery getter. Impressive. The car has certainly benefitted from the constant modifying and massaging from Nathan and Dave.

As we passed a small market, we noticed two vintage touring cars, a Model T and another car, in the parking lot. One was being worked on. We decided to stop and see if they needed a hand.

"Hey, you're the guys driving the Model T across the country," said a voice from beneath one of the cars. "I've been following you on the Internet."

Amazing. Here we were more than 3,000 miles from home, and a stranger working underneath his car was able to identify us!

"We're having fuel-pump issues on this Dodge," he said. "I'm installing an electric unit on it now so I can join the rest of our friends on a tour."

Dave gave him some helpful advice and we were back on our way.

About an hour later, we pulled into the parking lot of West Coast Metal Shaping, which is run by a young man named Andy Sucio. Dave was eager to meet Andy, who specialized in building metal bodies for hundred-year-old cars. This young man has become involved in the ancient art of metal working; he specializes in building the complex vintage bodies of speedsters and race cars. In his shop, he showed us some examples of his work.

Dave had heard about Andy because he was building a replica of a Laurel, a modified Model T speedster built in the early 1900s. Nathan had recently restored a Laurel at White Post Restorations, the shop where he works in Virginia.

I've always been amazed how some talented people can take a piece of flat metal and, through shrinking and stretching and rolling, can make it curl and bend in complex curves to nearly any shape. Andy studied under Fay Butler, a legend in the metal-crafting industry who mentors younger enthusiasts in this lost art.

Dave had made arrangements to visit the metal shop of Andy Sucio, a metalworker who is fabricating metal bodies for vintage cars. He learned his craft from one of California's master metal shapers.

"Many of the machines I have were purchased from my mentor, who is downsizing," Andy said.

"This machine is called a Pettingell," he said as he pointed out one of the large contraptions on his shop floor. "It's a power hammer that I'm told was built in the teens and originally used in the Duesenberg factory in Indiana."

Andy currently has three speedsters under construction for customers.

It is encouraging to see a young guy embracing this lost art form, something I would consider sculpture. The masters of this trade mostly came out of the L.A. area, where many were employed by the World War II aircraft industry. At night and on weekends, these same workers built hot rods, customs, dry-lake racers, and Indianapolis 500 cars and bodies.

That generation of metal workers are rapidly leaving us, but thankfully a few young guys have made it their life's goal to carry on the tradition.

20. Leaving Andy's shop, we reentered Highway 50. Remember Highway 50, the Loneliest Road in America? Well, it wasn't very lonely in California—it was absolutely crawling with traffic. What a contrast this was to the roads of Nevada just a couple of days earlier that had had virtually no speed limit.

Not needing to be anywhere at any special time, we just crawled along in the Sunday-afternoon rush hour. Not that we had any choice about it. About 100 miles was all that separated us from the Golden Gate Bridge, and according to Michael we'd have daylight until 8:15 p.m., so we had plenty of time.

There are a couple of Lincoln Highway routes through this section of California toward San Francisco. One is the I-80 route, which would bring us across the Golden Gate Bridge from the north, and the other is I-50 to the I-405, which would bring us up through Oakland and Berkeley from the south. We decided to take the I-80 route and approach our destination through Vallejo.

We had two missions to accomplish before sunset: photograph *Something* at the terminus of the Lincoln Highway in Lincoln Park and find a boat ramp so we could dip the wheels into Pacific waters. That would signify the official end of our trip.

I-80 was flowing nicely, allowing us to maintain a speed of 57 miles per hour.

21. It was warm, 90 degrees, and we were wringing every bit of speed out of *Something*. If we drove this car conservatively at the beginning of our trip, we were certainly putting her through its paces on this last leg.

Dave noticed the mercury on the radiator-mounted thermometer was, for the first time on this trip, visible. That meant the engine was getting hot, so we pulled off the highway to add some coolant.

OPPOSITE: The three of us had accomplished what many enthusiasts only dream of. Michael (left), who is seldom featured in the photos of this book, was a terrific partner in this journey. Dave and I thank you, Michael.

The dash-mounted thermometer, which had read as low as 28 degrees just two days ago, was registering 92 degrees.

Dave added additional coolant and we were on our way again. We decided to lower our speed to 49 miles per hour, hoping to keep the engine temperature cooler on the hot day. The cockpit temperature gauge rose to 94 degrees.

We exited the highway in Dixon and filled our fuel tank. This would likely be our final fill-up on the trip. While I was filling the tank, Michael came up to me.

"Do you know how hot it was back there in Sacramento?" he asked.

"Yeah," I said. "Our thermometer said 92 degrees."

"Try 100 degrees, buddy."

He was probably correct, since the digital thermometer in his 2017 SUV was likely more accurate, or at least better calibrated, than the ninety-two-year-old version that had been staring at me for the past fifteen days. That meant the temperature variance over the course of the trip had been 72 degrees! How do you pack the right clothes for a spread like that? (Actually, our clothing was always a compromise—never quite warm or cool enough, but always good enough.)

Fuel:
201.72 GALLONS
Distance:
3,625 MILES

We were nursing *Something* along on this final stretch, probably 50 miles from our destination. As we tooled along for those final few miles, it seemed like a good time to reflect on the past two weeks. *Something* had given us zero mechanical problems on the entire 3,000-plus-mile drive—we even had to fake a breakdown for photographic purposes. This is an amazing statement about a nearly century-old vehicle that had been driven faster, harder, and longer than Henry Ford ever imagined when he designed it more than a century ago.

It is a testament to Ford's vision of what a horseless carriage could be: basic, no-frills transportation that is well built and reliable. This car was certainly that and more.

22. Traffic was heavy, moving along at only 10 to 15 miles per hour, and the thermometer registered 100 degrees. The engine was starting to make ugly noises. Dave started turning the ignition switch on and off, allowing the car to coast as much as possible.

We were exhausted, but I sensed that *Something* wanted to get to the finish line even worse than we did.

Renowned race-car designer Colin Chapman built his Lotus cars so that they would theoretically fall apart at the finish line. The idea was that if a race car lasted any longer, it was overbuilt and therefore too heavy. Perhaps *Something* had a little bit of Lotus in her, because the Golden Gate was almost within sight and we were sweating bullets that we'd make it.

Come on, *Something*, don't fail us now.

Just as we were approaching the city of Vallejo, a couple of State Troopers—CHIPS, if you will—started weaving back and forth across the highway. They were obviously attempting to get every motorist's attention, And they ultimately brought traffic to a halt.

We sat there on the four-lane highway at 0 miles per hour, not realizing that there was a wreck ahead. Once it was cleared, we were grooving along at 50 again.

The ambient cockpit temperature had dropped to 90 degrees.

Coming over the ridge into Vallejo, we caught a clear view of the water to the west. A moment later, I could see the twin towers of the Golden Gate Bridge, still a mile away, but visible in the foggy distance.

We were on the homestretch, baby!

Fuel:
205.22 GALLONS
Distance:
3,688 MILES

23. Approaching the bridge from the west we were right down at sea level, with water on both sides of the road. The temperature was a pleasant 80 degrees and dropping. It felt good, and the salty smell was like a magic potion for we three weary travelers who hadn't smelt ocean air in a couple of weeks.

We had thought our last fuel stop would have been our final, but traffic west and southbound was so heavy toward the Golden Gate that we decided to make one more stop, get a drink of water, and sit in the shade for a few minutes. Dave took the opportunity to crawl under the car and adjust the transmission bands one more time. It felt good just to chill for a few minutes.

Since Michael actually lives nearby in San Raphael, he took us through all the back roads so we could avoid the heavy traffic on Highway 101. Suddenly it was getting cold—we were not yet at the bridge, and the temperature had fallen to 60 degrees and was still dropping. This was accompanied by heavy fog and a strong wind. My T-shirt and shorts were no longer sufficient.

We made it! Dave and I congratulate each other on this amazing accomplishment! It has been an incredible two weeks.

24. The first time I visited this area was in 1978 when I drove cross-country with my wife, Pat—then married just two years—in our rebuilt 1971 Datsun 240Z. We camped every night in a small pup tent and cooked our food on a camp stove. Our destination was Point Reyes National Seashore, where we planned to camp for a couple of days as we explored San Francisco and the surrounding area.

We had arrived during a heat wave, and the daytime temperatures were more than 112 degrees. In order to prevent the car from overheating, we drove with the heater on, therefore providing one more cooling radiator, the car's heater core, to help cool the car—and burn our legs. That was an ugly experience I still remember vividly forty years later.

To make matters worse, at night when we were setting up camp, I brushed against some stinging nettles, a plant I had never seen or heard of prior. It put me in painful misery for a couple of days.

I was hoping this trip to that region would be less dramatic.

. . . .

25.

Suddenly, there it was: the Golden Gate Bridge, with its towers partially hidden by the fog.

The Sunday traffic was still creeping along. Michael said that these were all Bay Area people who had spent the beautiful weekend up north in Napa Valley or Lake Tahoe. Now they were driving home to prepare for the work week, which would begin in the morning.

Michael had driven reconnaissance on this route a few weeks ago, so we let him lead the way as we followed.

Certainly we were not the first people to drive a Model T across the Unites States, but it's no longer an everyday occurrence. As we drove across, with the decal on our rear trunk there for all to see—"California or Bust"—it felt pretty special. We were within moments of the finish line.

We crossed the bridge and took the very first exit toward Lincoln Park.

We were there, at the western terminus of the Lincoln Highway. The three of us shared a few emotional moments with a big group hug at the concrete marker. Three guys in an emotional hug might grab attention in Georgia, but this was San Francisco, after all, and probably not the only time local bystanders had seen men hug that day.

It had been an amazing fourteen and a half days. The Lincoln Highway had been an amazing road, and *Something* had been an amazing car. And I traveled with two amazing partners, Dave and Michael. Dave and I spent two weeks sitting an inch away from one another. We talked, we looked, and we laughed. We learned about our country and each other, but mostly we spoke about *Something* in particular and cars in general—with a little bit of conversation about nuclear energy (Dave's passion) now and then.

I learned about cars, engines, and handling from this guy, who is a mechanical genius. He and car owner Nathan Edwards both worked on

Something nights and weekends leading up to the trip, prepping the engine and brakes and installing the new interior: seats, door panels, and side curtains.

26.
We had one more thing to do before we could retire to a bar to celebrate our accomplishment.

As had been a tradition in the earliest days of cross-country motoring, we had "baptized" *Something*'s tires in the Atlantic at the beginning of our journey in order to give the car, and us, good luck. Now we wanted to end the trip by doing the same in the Pacific. Weeks earlier, Michael had scoped out a boat ramp near what appeared to be an old Coast Guard Station, so we drove over and gave *Something* a bath.

It's something all of us needed, desperately.

ABOVE: We had made it to the West Coast. Now we just needed to figure out how to get *Something* back home to Virginia . . .

FOLLOWING PAGES: Certainly baptizing our tires before we left the New York metro area had given us good luck on this journey. Our trip was not officially completed until we duplicated the ritual by dipping *Something*'s tires into the Pacific Ocean.

Rage Against the Machine

....

Three months after the Model T trip, I needed to drive a modern vehicle from New England to Idaho, and I didn't have too much time. So I got on the interstate—first I-80, then I-90, then I-94—set the cruise control, and just motored down the road.

I slept in generic hotels, ate in modern restaurants, and scooted down the road at 80 miles per hour. In contrast to the Model T trip, I was able to commute in a matter of hours what had taken days in the T. But it was at a loss of intimacy. I met absolutely nobody on my 3,200-mile journey. It was sad, and quite a contrast to the slow road I had recently driven.

It made me glad I did have the opportunity to drive *Something* just a few months earlier. I was able to experience a disappearing slice of America that most travelers (including me on that recent trip) are denied.

I remember as a kid reading a futurist account of what American life would be like a couple of hundred years in the future. It predicted that everything a human being could want—food, clothing, entertainment— would be delivered with just the push of a button. In fact, the writer said that one day humans would be born without legs because it wouldn't be necessary to walk anywhere at all.

As a ten-year-old, I laughed at the notion. *No way*, I thought.

But with the advent of Amazon, literally anything you want can be delivered to your doorstep—books, clothing, vegetables. With a laptop or a phone, we can read any book in the world from anywhere in the world, making trips to the library or bookstore unnecessary. With Google, no matter where you are, the answer to nearly any question you could have is at your fingertips. So whether you are building a dog house, fileting a salmon, or rebuilding a Porsche 911 engine, your best friend is your computer screen, where you can get step-by-step instructions.

These easy solutions, though, raise the question of whether it is necessary to actually learn anything anymore. In the future, in addition to rebuilding a Porsche engine, will a neophyte be able to perform open-heart surgery?

The actual function of handwriting, whether printed or cursive, is becoming a lost art. Because writing is so seldom done these days, with most people using the keyboard either on their mobile device or on a computer, school administrators are questioning whether students should even be taught the art of handwriting and penmanship anymore.

I just discovered that a pencil store has opened in New York's swanky East Side where customers can shop for everything from basic pencils, for as little as 35 cents each, to vintage pencils, for as much as $75. The business in the rapidly disappearing art of actually writing is said to be booming, but it's more for novelty purposes than an everyday practice.

At the end of the day, self-driving cars are as much our future as horses and buggies were our past. With all the distractions that motorists deal with—texting, conversations, GPS— it's probably a good thing. Hopefully the death and injury rate on US highways will rapidly decline as a result.

But this increased safety comes at the loss of personal freedom. Cars are becoming transportation pods that passengers will walk into, enter their destination, then go about their digital business—watch movies, have phone conversations, text, sleep—and somehow arrive safe and sound at the correct location.

I can't get the image of the orgasmatron from Woody Allen's 1973 movie *Sleeper* out of my mind. In the movie, consenting couples in the future would enter a windowless pod that looked like a phone booth (remember those?) and, without touching each other, would achieve . . . well, you know. No muss, no fuss, no undressing. In a matter of moments, they were back to their daily tasks.

It's funny in a Woody Allen science-fiction comedy, but is that the direction we want to go in with the automobile? Not me.

Self-driving cars will make nearly instantaneous decisions to avoid accidents. And these new modes of transport will make our trips more efficient by routing passengers (I hesitate to call them drivers, motorists, or operators) on the shortest, most efficient roads to get from Point A to Point B.

But for all the positive changes self-driving cars can bring us, they can't help us make friends. Travelers in the near future will be riding on generic highways, staying in generic hotels and eating generic food next to other generic travelers. The idea of travel as a romantic endeavor will be

over forever. Never again will travelers meet Sandy, who managed the Colo Restaurant, or Matt and Maya in Emigrant Pass in California, or receive one of Darrell and Rosie Crouse's good luck "nuts." And that will be a bloody shame.

Those of a certain mindset will allow the future to direct their lives, but some of us need to balk at that suggestion.

If you act quickly, there is still time to take one last road trip. But you must hurry, because the clock is ticking. Soon driving, like the experience of the orgasmatron, will become an antiseptic activity.

HAPPY TRAILS,
TOM COTTER

Photographer's Notes

....

As I've worked with Tom Cotter through what is now our fifth book together, I've learned to never underestimate his knack for coming up with the next wacky, wonderful concept.

Traveling cross-country in a '26 Ford Model T just didn't quite seem doable. And even when we decided to go for it, the nagging possibility of the myriad things that could go wrong wouldn't leave me. But adding Dave Coleman (driver, builder, ace mechanic, and Model T expert) to the mix helped me get past my own doubts.

Picking up Tom at the airport, I realized this would be our last drive in the same car until we reached San Francisco. The next morning, Tom and Dave climbed into the Model T, and I was solo, driving the support vehicle, acting as their back bumper for the next several thousand miles.

I was the photographer, shuttle driver, and damage-control specialist, with my trigger finger on the four-way flashers at any moment. I was the last to show up at every stop and the last to leave. The rules were easy. We were all traveling west on the same road. If we were to get separated at any time, just keep heading west, and that's what we did. From sunup to sundown for fourteen days at an average speed of 52 miles per hour.

There were times when I would go batty just watching that little T in the lane in front of me hour after hour, day after day. Other times, I'd be trying desperately to catch up if I had lost them at a light or intersection.

As the miles went on, I began to realize that if I were to photograph some of these great vistas with the car in them, I was going to have to figure out a way to shoot while we were still moving. There was no way these guys were going to stop for me. So what I decided to do is activate the adaptive cruise control and set the distance control so I could lock in on the speed and exact distance from the Model T. Of course, shooting through the tinted windshield had an adverse effect on the look of the images. So I would open the sunroof and hold the camera up with one hand (and the other on the steering wheel). At speed, this is not an easy task, and it defies aerodynamics, to say the least.

After firing a few bursts, I would check to see how close I was to getting the Model T in focus. With patience and the wonders of modern technology (both the camera's and that of the 2017 Ford Escape I was driving) I was able to get the shots. Of course, I wouldn't recommend this to anyone, and please note that this was always done on a two-lane with no oncoming traffic.

Mile after mile, the topography changed, and with every change, a different photo op. We went from the heart of NYC to the Wild Wild West and saw everything in between. We met stranger after stranger and left friend after friend all along the way. That little Model T put a smile on everyone's face. No one could believe we were making this trip, and you could see they were envious.

As I always tell my wife while pitching yet another one of Tom's crazy ideas, who else gets to do this? Thanks again, Tom. This is another one we'll both be talking about for years to come.

MICHAEL ALAN ROSS

Bibliography

....

BOOKS

Anderson, Mary Elizabeth. *Link Across America*. 1997, Windsor, CA: Rayve Productions.

Brinkley, Douglas. *Wheels for the World*. 2003, New York: Viking Press.

Bryson, Bill. *The Lost Continent*. 1989, New York: Harper and Row.

Buck, Rinker. *Flight of Passage*. 1997, New York: Hachette Books.

Butko, Brian. *Greetings from the Lincoln Highway*. 2005, Mechanicsburg, PA: Stackpole Books.

Casey, Robert. *The Model T: A Centennial History*. 2008, Baltimore, MD: Johns Hopkins University Press.

Clymer, Floyd. *Henry's Wonderful Model T*. New York: Bonanza Books.

Davies, Pete. *American Road*. 2002, New York: Henry Holt.

Duncan, Dayton and Ken Burns. *Horatio's Drive*. 2003, New York: Borzoi Books.

Kerouac, Jack. *On the Road*. 1959, New York: Penguin Books.

Lacey, Robert. *Ford: The Men and the Machine*. 1986, New York: Ballantine Books.

Least Heat-Moon, William. *Blue Highways*. 1982, New York: Little, Brown and Company.

Maxim, Hiram Percy. *Horseless Carriage Days*. 1936, 1962, Mineola, NY: Dover Publications.

Sommer Simmons, Christine. *The American Motorcycle Girl's Cannonball Diary*. 2012, Parker House.

Steinbeck, John. *Travels with Charlie*. 1961, Philadelphia, PA: Curtis Publishing Company.

Wallis, Michael and Michael S. Williamson *The Lincoln Highway*. 2007, New York: W.W. Norton & Company.

Wilson, Paul C. *Chrome Dreams*. 1976, Chilton Book Company.

WEB SOURCES

Atlas Obscura atlasobscura.com

Eisenhower Presidential Library eisenhower.archives.gov

Ohio History Central ohiohistorycentral.org

Index

· · · · · · · · · · · · ·

Before writing his first book, **TOM COTTER** had long been involved in nearly every end of the automotive and racing industries. From mechanic and auto salesman to heading the public relations department at Charlotte Motor Speedway, Cotter formed his own racing and automotive PR and marketing agency, Cotter Group. The agency represented some of the largest clients in NASCAR, IndyCar/CART, drag racing and road racing. He has written biographies of the legendary Holman-Moody race team, Tommy Ivo and Dean Jeffries, but is best known for his series of barn find books, such as *Cobra in the Barn*, *50 Shades of Rust*, and *Motor City Barn Finds*. Cotter appears in the Barn Find Hunter YouTube video series, which is produced by Hagerty Insurance. He teaches public relations at Belmont Abbey College, sits on the advisory board of McPherson College's Auto Restoration program, and is a member of the Road Racing Driver's Club (RRDC). He is married to Pat, has one car-crazy son, Brian, and lives in Davidson, NC.

Embodied with a passion for all things automotive, **MICHAEL ALAN ROSS** has carved out a career photographing the studied nuances, latest models, adrenaline-rushed raceways and proud owners of the car world. His love of car design includes an encyclopedic knowledge of sculptural engineering details, with a parallel appreciation for the evolution of a component and a sentimentality for the classics. Inspired by his respect for the craftsmanship of car designers, Michael draws upon their influence as a narrative for his work—the parts and pieces, technological advances and elements that capture a moment in time.